AN UNKNOWN DESTINY

AN UNKNOWN
DESTINY

Terror, Psychotherapy, and Modern Initiation:
Readings in Nietzsche, Heidegger, Steiner

MICHAEL GRUBER

Foreword by Robert Sardello, Ph.D.

LINDISFARNE BOOKS
2008

LINDISFARNE BOOKS
AN IMPRINT OF STEINERBOOKS / ANTHROPOSOPHIC PRESS
610 MAIN STREET, GREAT BARRINGTON, MA 01230
www.steinerbooks.org

Library of Congress Cataloging-in-Publication Data

Gruber, Michael.
    An unknown destiny : terror, psychotherapy, and modern initiation:
readings in Nietzsche, Heidegger, Steiner / Michael Gruber.
      p. cm.
    ISBN 978-1-58420-064-2
    1. Terrorism. 2. Terrorism–Psychological aspects. 3. Psychic trauma.
4. Psychotherapy. 5. Nietzsche, Friedrich Wilhelm, 1844-1900. 6.
Heidegger, Martin, 1889-1976. 7. Steiner, Rudolf, 1861-1925. I. Title.
    B105.T47G78 2008
      193–dc22

                          2008037449

PRINTED IN THE UNITED STATES

Contents

Acknowledgments   vii
List of Abbreviations   xi
Foreword by Robert Sardello, Ph.D.   xiii

Introduction   1
1. From Ornithology to a Love Supreme: Overcoming the
   Forces of Gravity, and the Teaching of *Amor Fati*   17

2. Zarathustra's Convalescence: Cognitive Expansions
   and Inner Wisdom   38

3. With Nietzsche on the Road from Revenge to
   Redemption   53

4. Traumatic Pain: Psychotherapeutic Conversation
   Between Mediumship and Soul Wisdom   69

5. Psychotherapy as a Vocation: Giving Voice to Soul   90

6. Intuitive and Inceptual Thinking: The Meditative
   Paths of Steiner and Heidegger   109

7. "While My Conscience Explodes"...   127

Literature Cited   151
Index   157

Acknowledgments

For providing me with the solitude and sustenance necessary to complete this book, I wish to express my gratitude to those who have encouraged, facilitated, and validated my efforts.

Since arriving in New York City over thirty years ago to attend graduate school at the New School for Social Research, I have been most fortunate to participate in an invigorating and ongoing conversation about sociocultural matters—and to share a close friendship—with Alan Mandell. An innovative adult educator with a deep commitment to dialogue and ethics, Alan has been a deep pool of contemplative kindness and a more-than-competent player of "surrender and catch." And, during times when various forms of terror have threatened me with personal or intellectual derailment, he has provided thoughtful conversation, steadfast support, and many holiday dinners. To supplement the emotional insufficiency of "thank you," I offer a quiet bow.

Much of my psychological education, both as a person and as a therapist, has occurred within an imaginal alchemical vessel provided by Nathan Schwartz-Salant. I am deeply indebted to him for granting me the possibility to experience and experiment with the *solve et coagulae* process that is at the heart of individuation and transformation. Through our sharing of many of my often chaotic dreamscapes, I have come to better appreciate the creativity of the unconscious. Perhaps most profoundly, our work together has taught me that healthy relationships require not only receptive listening and careful attention, but also a space where being-for-the-other shelters vulnerability.

To the Friday afternoon Frog Medicine Group, especially to Mark Reich, where much of the thinking contained in this book received its early articulation, much warmth.

Through numerous psycho-geographic journeys, in silence and in speech, Mary Rose Donahue has always been a supportive voice. I send her deep positive energies.

Consciously or not, a book is always looking for a home and a receptive host. From the inception of this work, Christopher Bamford has offered unconditional welcome, enthusiastic guidance, and a generous sharing of ideas. I have gained immeasurably from his commitment to the attainment of knowledge, especially the caring and critical way he approaches the revelation of the unknown and his pursuit of the "traces" that hint at and point toward the elusiveness of truth. Always a stimulating interlocutor, during our talks Chris has opened paths of thinking and relating to me that unequivocally demonstrate that "An act of hospitality can only be poetic" (Jacques Derrida).

To Gene Gollogly and the staff at SteinerBooks, thank you for providing a first-time author a convivial forum to express ideas that had remained in my study too long.

I have been exceedingly privileged to have the editorial help of Sarah J. Gallogly, a devotee of clarity with a musical ear for language. Sarah's insistence that communication can retain a poetics of communion and need not deteriorate into jargon or empty prose prodded me to seek for the *logos*. Whether I have succeeded in this search is ultimately my responsibility, but whatever merits this book has would be diminished without her committed and lively help.

While the case studies that have almost become obligatory when talking about psychotherapy are absent from this book, I would be more than negligent if I avoided thanking those individuals and couples who have engaged me in conversation and risked speaking their agonies and joys. In this exposure of much that has been and continues to be terrifying, I have learned that patience is a virtue and that patients who attend faithfully to the unknown in their souls are rewarded with lives that contain new meaningfulness.

Ultimately, the other who is one's closest intimate reveals the profound unknown of one's destiny. My wife, Leah, has participated in this book, often as an astute reader and commentator, but more frequently as a generative force whose openness to new ideas has led me to pursue paths of thinking that at first appeared less than promising. More importantly, her emotional wholesomeness and ethical integrity have inspired me to face my own doubts and fears and to engage in previously unimaginable transformations. Leah, your playfulness and tenacity inspire me. Blessings.

List of Abbreviations

Works by Friedrich Nietzsche

AC   *The Anti-Christ*
BGE   *Beyond Good and Evil*
EH   *Ecce Homo*
Z   *Thus Spoke Zarathustra*

Works by Martin Heidegger

BQ   *Basic Questions of Philosophy*
BT   *Being and Time*
CP   *Contributions to Philosophy (From Enowning)*
DT   *Discourse on Thinking*
EHP   *Elucidations of Hölderlin's Poetry*
LH   *Letter on Humanism*
EP   *End of Philosophy*
M   *Mindfulness*
PLT   *Poetry, Language, Thought*
QT   *The Question Concerning Technology and Other Essays*

Foreword

NEW PSYCHOLOGIES spring up nearly as fast as new model cars. Each of them bears pretty much the same assumptions. There is something from the past, not fully conscious, that must be dissolved, eliminated, eradicated, and maybe forgiven, if one is to feel comfortable within the world. Other forms of therapy—concern for the soul, connecting with archetypal realities, awakening a sense of Self—exist only at the outer margins of culture. The more common and more universal view of therapeutic psychology degrades the "Queen of Disciplines" into a primarily pragmatic technology oriented toward restoring individuals to being servants of the collective realm, the masses, the State. Radically put, Michael Gruber convincingly shows us that psychology has become the servant of terrorist structures of consciousness.

We are primarily aware of the physical dimensions of terrorism and are wholly oriented toward strategies of war against it: terrorism fighting terrorism. We remain totally unaware of how the dominant mode of spectator consciousness—in which we become onlookers not only on the world, but also on ourselves—turns destructive at a certain point in the evolution of consciousness because of the inevitable unfolding of the primacy of power and control. That point has forcefully arrived. We have become free and independent (or act as if we are) of the spiritual forces of nature and of the cosmos and seemingly become the creators of our own human destiny.

The formation of the egoic structure of consciousness is responsible for this illusion, an illusion that substitutes self-centeredness for individuality of being. By this I mean the notion of having the right to be an independent entity rather than feeling the mysterious individuality of human life in its ongoing currents within the undisclosed mystery of Being. This illusion is upheld through all-pervasive intrinsic fear, which results in the construction both of a world of distractions to veil the fear and defenses that keep it from being exposed. As a consequence, a doubling of egoic consciousness has come about that has made it possible to manipulate fear as the instrument to perpetuate control within the system of this dominant structure of consciousness. The control comes about by turning everything—even intangible realities—into something to be commodified, placing it within an imagination of need and of scarcity that keeps attention occupied with the "outside" and the fantasy that inner peace is attained through outer satisfaction.

Michael Gruber shows us, in magnificent ways, that the only way through the age of terror is through taking up forms of modern initiatory practices. This path of knowledge is led, surprisingly, not by spiritual leaders and initiates, but is undertaken through self-initiation founded in the felt sense that soul and spirit must always be entered simultaneously and without detaching from the world. Spiritual practices alone lead to various sorts of mania, while soul practices alone lead to self-absorption. In our time, spirituality and psychology must merge into a creative synthesis of spiritual psychology if we are to break through into new structures of consciousness.

Spiritually oriented psychology frees us from an obsessive, singular view toward the past, which can serve only to keep the focus on what is done, completed, and perpetuates a closed system, unable to find the truly new. Such spiritual psychology is a creative rather than a destructive explosion, opening the closed system of consciousness into the emergence, within ongoing life, of the practical workings of divine forces that compose both the world and the human being, both intrinsically one and expressed in a world-individual polarity. What we find in the world is always ourselves, spiritually displayed, and what we find individually is always the world in its signification.

Psychotherapy, understood in its most radical sense as the practice of the "Queen of Disciplines" concerns initiation, an insight that leads this book into extraordinary places. Psychotherapy, as intimated by Gruber, may be the only contemporary venue available for initiation. It is primarily a prototypal action between people, in which the vertical imagination that has characterized spiritual practices of the past is now found in the "between." This implies a revolution in the initiatory process, one in which the "gods" are no longer situated in the vertical "above" or "below." The gods have not completely disappeared, but now persist in the soul/spirit field between people. As long as this shift goes unrecognized, however, people still rely on dead religions for the shell of spiritual experience or on outmoded, atavistic kinds of spiritual practices that, at best, can take one only into a memory of the spiritual worlds, not its living presence all around us.

The trouble, of course, is that psychology is completely contaminated and can only impotently touch the outer surface of what is now available as soul/spirit experience. Indeed, psychology does not even recognize the autonomy of spirit experience and, at best, in a few of the depth psychologies, classifies spirit experience as a variety of soul or psychic experience, depriving it of the reality of imaginal realms and presences that are autonomous from human-being, but only disclosed and opened through human heart-presence. That is to say, psychology can, when it stretches real hard, understand human beings as having spiritual experiences, but it does not have the proper tools to understand what it is to be a spiritual human being and not simply a human being doing spiritual things.

In *An Unknown Destiny*, Gruber has written the prototypal book that gives us the basic new tools to undergo and recognize that humanity is passing through an as-yet unrecognized initiatory shift of being. It is extremely important to notice—well, one cannot help but notice—that this book is written in such a way that the whole of it is in every part; it all occurs simultaneously and it is only due to the limitations of having to put it into standard linear language, that it unfolds page by page. When reading this book it is important to feel that we have been invited into the intensity of meditative consciousness. While the form of the writing takes us through essentials of the work of Nietzsche, Heidegger, and Steiner, it is no mere exposition of or commentary on what these individuals thought and did. The writing is already within a new mode or octave of consciousness. Having to struggle within this new form brings about at least the beginning of the formation of new capacities. It is a book to undergo rather than simply to read. It is a book to bear, as in bearing a new child.

I have never been particularly fond of Nietzsche, probably because I saw many of my fellow students, years ago, taken, fascinated, even entranced, with his passion, but with no way to let that passion open into something creative. At last that view changes here. A central effect of Gruber's creative approach to Nietzsche, is to demonstrate, not simply talk about, the fact that it is necessary to throw oneself across the threshold into initiatory realms, into the completely unknown. Initiatory experience cannot be planned; one cannot, in advance, know where one is going or what will happen. Even more, this chopping off of one's purposive, calculating head must be done with the greatest enthusiasm possible. Still, why choose Nietzsche to exemplify this necessity? Part of the answer lies in suggesting that Nietzsche's program for abandoning our mental structures is exactly what is needed to enter the unknown and to develop the capacity of letting life unfold from the unknown, unknowingly, and with the fullest attention.

A further response lies in Zarathustra, Nietzsche's Zarathustra. Living intimately within the soul-being of Nietzsche was—no, is—the paradigm of fully bodied imaginal consciousness. And Zarathustra is additionally paradigmatic of present-day initiate consciousness, which includes an awareness of the massive tendency always to reduce the human being and world-being to the reductive "nothing-but" category of material processes, wholly subject to the intense cleverness of sub- and unconscious presences that seem deep and mysterious—even the realm of the gods— but are in fact hell-bent on making hell seem as if it were paradise.

The entry point and wholeness of the initiation of humanity is to be found in developing the capacity of imaginal consciousness. This book is written wholly from within imaginal consciousness. Michael Gruber tells us from the outset that a different and wholly unfamiliar structure of thinking is needed to enter into the next stage of consciousness and that this structure is "heart-thinking," which gives access to the imaginal realms. Here, then, is the key to the whole of what this book is about and the reason why it is not possible to read this work without undergoing inner change.

Heart-thinking consists of taking in, in a completely receptive manner, what is before one—sensory experience, or ideas, or images and even dreams—not mentally, but through reaching out through the heart to feel their presence as the interiority of Being, and even as the traces of spirit presences. Feeling is something active. It is not simply the inner reaction to something. We feel—as in "to reach out and touch." The interior heart region is the only bodily region capable of this reaching out to touch that is accompanied with a particular kind of consciousness— the consciousness of the inner presence of the inner qualities of what we attend to. What we attend to in this manner echoes within us. Then it fades gradually, like the afterimage of a candle. The fading, however, is not the disappearance of what was received; rather, what was received now finds its way into the larger cosmos; it finds its connection with spiritual presences. Then, the Whole is felt as inner resonance and can be expressed as intuitive insights. This way of knowing is a new yoga; it is what Rudolf Steiner called "the new yoga of Light." It is our access to imaginal consciousness; it is the way through dualistic, separative consciousness.

The complete sense of what imaginal consciousness consists of has many dimensions. The dimension that is most clearly demonstrated in this writing is that this new form is a new orientation—one which is "situative" rather than "situated." Rather than speaking of something as if it is already formed and completed, as we do when stringing thoughts together, this mode of consciousness enters the unknown in the deepest of Silence, and waits with full attention until something wants to be said. It is a thinking-together with spiritual presences. We feel, then, something coming-into-being, situating, rather than as already here to be described as a dead corpse. We always feel such situative thinking as inspired, brilliant, new, creative. And true. Such is the way of this book.

Central to imaginal consciousness, and thus to Zarathustra—and through him, Nietzsche—is the complete engagement of the gods, of God, with the human. God seeks to be known, longs to be known by human beings, for this is the way God knows God. The engagement between the gods and humans is a kind of play in which one becomes the other, and the un-manifest continually becomes manifest. None of this vast complex unity is available to usual consciousness. Entry is gained through attending to the longing of the heart, gradually recognizing that this longing is not ours, not our wanting to fulfill some need or desire, but is the presence of God's longing for us. Developing the capacity to follow the presence of longing into new forms of consciousness requires becoming present to the creative capacity of attention. Attention is not just noticing something, letting something get hold of our attention; rather it is the creative, generative spiritual organ through which the presence of the workings of forces beyond us can be felt as intimately engaged with us. Through developing attentive presence, transformations of the heart ensue, reconfiguring the whole we are and are within.

Equally central to being present to the imaginal is that we run into the opposing forces of darkness, those necessary beings that are impediments to smooth sailing in imaginal realms when that sailing is also world-oriented. One would think that having discovered heart-thinking, where even thinking itself is felt as a cooperative endeavor with spiritual presences, would open a new and beautiful world. It does, but that does not rid either us or the world of the impulses of revenge, violence, cleverness, and forgetfulness that now dominate earthly materialistic consciousness. Now, however, the context is quite different. At least potentially, a modicum of freedom is present in which it becomes possible to attain a creative presence with these delicious darknesses. Nietzsche, in the end, however, may well have been swallowed by them through the fatal wound of his own hubris or *amor fati*. Thus, something more is needed than the leap into engagement.

Although Nietzsche participated deeply in the felt realization that consciousness itself is formed of and by love—and in the living of *amor fati*—he still manifests a certain thrashing about. There is still present in him a blending of love and passion, and a felt-sense of presences without the capacity of truly allowing and perceiving their autonomy within a unity of consciousness. Rudolf Steiner, the second presiding genius engaged by Michael Gruber, had enormous respect for Nietzsche and even wrote a book about him, *Nietzsche: Fighter for Freedom*. Steiner recognized in Nietzsche the beginnings of heart-thinking. Thus, it is not surprising to find these two, Nietzsche and Steiner, side by side in this book. The chapters on Steiner are a remarkable synthesis of Steiner's enormous gifts to the world; while the sections on psychotherapy are of particular importance in recognizing psychotherapy as a modern initiation practice.

The kind of therapy suggested in the Steiner section of this writing is an excursion across the border into the land of the unknown. What a therapist needs to develop far more than any theoretical knowledge or techniques is the capacity of complete surrender. Surrender does not just happen. It is not just a kind of giving up, or letting go. Rather, it is an active process, a conscious process of yielding into an unknown that is something more than an absence, a void, but is an opening to a resonating presence of a field that encompasses both therapist and patient. Some depth psychologists are familiar with this field and have written and theorized about it as the "interactive field." Michael Gruber adds significantly to our knowledge of this realm, first by noting that being within this field of the "third" requires a pouring of all of attention into the field so that nothing is left as observer or even as witness. Further, this yielding into the field that has captured the patient in overwhelming ways—that simultaneously threaten and announce freedom of being—is nothing less than an excursion into the land of death without a map. It is entirely reminiscent of descriptions of spiritual awakening and its attending dangers.

A brilliant sketch of the new territory of therapeutic initiation is given that, in its detail, shows that initiatory experiences, which are now happening spontaneously to many people, are typically put under the old classification of psychological illnesses. They are not psychological illness at all. They are spiritual rumblings that can happen within the emotional body, or the life body, or in the realms of character, wishes, desires, longing. Most significantly they are something that at once announces and thwarts the awaking possibility of developing the capacity of creative generation of oneself as world-relation at each moment. That is, what is now increasingly coming about in the world is the possibility to apprehend every moment as our coming-into-being rather than as "having" an identity, which may be threatened by the press of past difficulties.

The pathologies of new consciousness, a consciousness sensitive to and capable of receiving impressions from creative spiritual presences as well as destructive ones, are pathologies or sufferings of becoming rather than of having-been. Scratching around to locate the origin of such suffering in the past—and even in the archetypal rather than the prototypal imagination—serves only to feed the darkness. Obsessions with death and dying, chronic fatigue, attention deficit "disorders," terror of fragmentation, dissociating, certain kinds of delusion, and most significantly because it is now epidemic, bi-polar disorder, are illnesses that have to do with the real, substantial time stream from the future; illnesses of *potentia*, of coming-to be. Simply to be removed from the soul's be-coming due to living within a culture of the past, which is now "egotized," is already an illness. In addition, because there exists absolutely nothing in the culture that prepares and strengthens the heart forces for the influx of the coming-to-be, shatterings of the soul occur, due to the overwhelming experiences of this initiatory threshold that is now upon humanity. This book is utterly groundbreaking and courageous in bringing these new pathologies to light. Furthermore, these new sufferings require completely new senses of the practice of psychotherapy and the training of therapists. As long as therapists are educated in old ways, the revelations of these sufferings remain closed.

An additional factor enters when experiences of suffering related to being overwhelmed in the dimension of coming-to-be occur within a culture dominated by technicity and materialism. Under these conditions, these experiences often do not show up as sufferings at all, but rather as the capacity to inflict suffering, especially terrorizing trauma, on others without any feeling or comprehension of the moral depravity involved. This tricky situation is due to the process of doubling. Doubling was first recognized as a pathology by Robert Jay Lifton, though there are many precedents of the phenomenon in literature, such as the writing of Guy de Maupassant. I have traced out this heritage in my book, *Freeing the Soul from Fear*. Nowadays, however, what was an unusual phenomenon of seeing oneself before oneself—doing things that one would never do

(Jekyl and Hyde, is an example of this phenomenon)—has taken a further step in development.

The individual spirit being of a person can be doubled by a force that looks, acts like, and seems to be one's spirit being. But it is taken over by cleverness and power. We see the phenomenon everywhere in corporate culture and in politics. It is a spiritual pathology, intensely difficult to break through because those bearing it are, within this culture, the highly successful. This book provides a first step in working with this illness in an extremely clear picturing of the various forms of doubling. This first step is thus to become aware of the phenomenon, to realize that there is an inherent incredible cleverness to doubling that cannot be countered, and then to be able to enter into a heart field with one who is experiencing the malady. Being within the field of the heart allows the phenomenon to open up in an attitude of wonder, and also involves including others who are connected with the individual be a part of the therapeutic work, and letting the field go into the laconic presence of death.

Modern therapeutic initiate consciousness does not take place inwardly, separated from the world. One way to grasp the overall structure of this book and why it is written the way it is—as a creative synthesis of the three figures of Nietzsche, Heidegger, and Steiner—is to see that, by entering their spiritual imaginations, we come to Wholeness. With Nietzsche, as presented here, we have the dimension of individual initiation as it can take place in the midst of a dead culture that refuses to recognize that it is dead and thus perpetuates destruction. The other polarity of individual initiation is world initiation. The earth, in its union with the human, has to be understood, felt, and experienced as not only living, but as conscious. The human being in this sense of the unity of earth-human is something entirely different than consciousness of earth. This unity is the dimension of being most clearly spoken by Heidegger; it is the aspect of the human world he was most concerned with. And in this context, it is Rudolf Steiner who seems to hold the polarity together in one unity, the unity of I-World.

As a way of helping to clarify the bridging capacity of Rudolf Steiner, we may note that his detailed esoteric description of the evolution of the world never separates the evolution of the earth from the evolution of the human being. It is not the usual picture of evolution, which acts as if the earth were finished and completed before the ape-to-become human mysteriously emerges from the protein soup—a fiction of science that does not recognize its fictionalizing.

Rudolf Steiner had capacities of clairvoyantly thinking with evolution, of re-living the entire process of evolution. To give one example of the polarity of person-world evolution, consider how Steiner speaks of the relation of gemstones to the human being. Gemstones came into being on the earth at the same time as the human was evolving into a sensory being. An intimate connection thus exists between gemstones and the human senses. According to Steiner, gems, when they were still fluid in form, were the presences of angelic beings, who participated in earth evolution to assure that as the human senses formed they would not become so completely earth-bound that humans would completely lose the capacity to experience something of the spiritual field through the senses. They represent a sacrifice of angelic beings, who now, in a way, remain here, as frozen memories of spirit activity. This may sound far-fetched, unless entered into as an imaginal picture, something like a myth—not myth as fiction, but myth as something that never really happened, but is always happening.

There is still a great inability to see and to feel the intimate ongoing connection between the earth and humans. Certainly, there is now the recognition that we can and are harming the earth, but we still live in a dualistic imagination, thinking and living as if the earth were other than us, rather than a polarity of human-world. Heidegger, I think it would be accurate to say, expresses at least part of this polarity-of-unity with the term "Being," though Being of course is even more than this. Heidegger, throughout his philosophy, decries the forgetfulness of Being. Michael Gruber, I think, intuitively sees that going to Heidegger brings out what may be more difficult to understand in Steiner; just as he goes to Nietzsche to bring out and emphasize and re-awaken the pull-to-freedom, which is the center of Steiner's work, but exists in a more pressing sense in Nietzsche.

Any spiritual psychology focusing on the human being without being able to develop a comprehensive imagination that includes the earth is doomed not only to failure, but operates out of the old consciousness that will be swallowed by darkness. Ekhart Tolle, for example, operates out of this kind of dualistic consciousness while trying to put forth a concern for the earth. As a consequence, what he says results in a kind of new age egoism. This evaluation does not intend any judgment of Tolle per se, but rather indicates the necessity of finding the way through terrorist structures of consciousness, no matter how appealing and "life-renewing" they might appear on the surface. Sadly, one of the great harbingers of terrorist structures of consciousness is to be found in much spiritual work and writing—that is, in spirituality of the type that has not found the way through dualistic consciousness and sees spirituality as something essentially private, inward, self-developmental, and, with world difficulties now so pressing, tries to add on to an egoistic mode of operation a concern for the world.

The chapter in this book on Heidegger is thus pivotal. The healing of the world cannot, as Gruber clearly states, be a matter of old consciousness with new content. We must develop the capacity to "think Being." "Being" sounds like a terribly abstract, philosophical term, not connected with experience. In fact, like true thinking it is an experience unavailable to anyone unable to get beyond the "me"—or even the "we." Thinking Being is an experience available meditatively, and is a "thinkingly" clear felt sense of the animated unity and complexity of all that is, directly apprehended. It is the return of the living sense of Mystery, something to behold, rather than something to be utilized. It is something to be listened to from within as a formative force. Doing so brings about a form of consciousness characterized by a different structure of thinking—meditative rather than calculative thinking. It is a structure of thinking that thinks along with the things of the world, rather than about them, allowing them to disclose their own meaning and purpose. This meaning and purpose is conveyed within a field of unity with the individual, as a felt imaginal presence. It is not something that can be apprehended through usual knowing, nor spoken in usual language, and it does not follow the laws of our logic. Thus, Heidegger devotes much of his writing on Being to the mystery of the poetic language that simultaneously reveals and conceals, and is essential to the primary creative act of dwelling.

The new initiatory therapy lives and breathes within this context of Mystery. It makes possible being completely and lovingly with someone within a field of un-knowing and wonder—not waiting for something to happen that will "solve" the mystery, uncover the hidden background from the past, but becoming available for disclosures that do not make logical sense, and are, rather, felt presences of the unfolding of an individual life in moments of harmony with that of others and the earth. In these moments, individual healing cannot be separated from the healing of the earth.

Because there is an aura of mystery and discovery that surrounds even present forms of therapy, most therapists are more than likely unaware that they function within a kind of calculative thinking. Working with feelings or dreams or images does not move one away from this disposition of thinking. Images, for example, are treated as "things" to be looked at, as ways in which the psyche reveals itself rather than as worlds to be entered together by therapist and patient, worlds that cannot be cognitively known and worlds that are far from personal and even far from the presence of archetypal worlds. The challenge of this book is to radicalize therapy, to see that all of psychology to this point has been nothing more than a preparatory and transitional discipline, a training of consciousness for modern initiation, which now takes place with others, rather than through one's solitary meditative practices. I hope that at least a few therapists will feel the truth of what Michael Gruber has written and take up the magnificent work that he proposes.

Robert Sardello, Ph.D.
Co-Director, The School of Spiritual Psychology

Introduction

Dangers and Opportunities

The questions I shall pursue in these pages concern the structures of human consciousness that dominated the organization of psychosocial and ecopolitical relationships during the twentieth century and continue to do so into the third millennium. Among the many signs testifying to the unique character of the present epoch, in which so many of our guideposts have fallen, we shall take as their most authoritative expression Friedrich Nietzsche's words: "God is dead." Appearing over a century ago in *The Gay Science* (1974, III, 125), this boldest of judgments confronts us as human beings with our own abolition of the Supreme Being and the loss of connection to divine guidance for how to live a moral life. As compensation for this atheological and demoralizing darkening, we have developed self-consciousness and a sense of freedom. But the price is a life lived at the boundary of the Void. Thus, occupying a life-world without commanding truths to anchor moral principles, we find ourselves facing a *rupture in human destiny*.

The rift caused by our condemnation of God encloses us in a sociopolitical order where appeals to religious sources of meaning and the adjudication of fate are rendered irrelevant. Unable to redeem our tragic lack of absolute principles by the "invention of festivals of atonement and sacred games" (Ibid.) through which we substitute self-deification for the divinities that we deny, we are now compelled to live our destiny outside of any transcendent framework.

Beyond the systematic discontent of civilization diagnosed—and contributed to—by Freud (1962), it is my contention that the *rupture in human destiny* over the past century has exposed us to an experience of perpetual *displacement*. The modern idea of progress is eroding our personal, geographic, and national identity and depriving us of the familiar references that give meaning to our being-in-the-world. Consequently, our destiny increasingly takes place in the absence of any fundamental teleology. Instead, it unfolds within highly structured and legitimated forms of psychosocial and political-economic life which are expressions of the all-encompassing worldview of our time: the *universalization of terror*.

Without recourse to the transcendent truths which began with the Sinaitic revelations and found philosophic expression in early Greek thought, we strive for meaning and survival within a materialistic universe where relentless military warfare devastates nations, the globalization of capitalism radically polarizes wealth and poverty, and fear proliferates into all areas of everyday experience. The need and the occasion to ask essentially ethical or metaphysical questions is being replaced with the obsession with control and security. Tolerating only secular and often amoral attitudes toward personal and social issues, the universalization of terror renders both public and private life increasingly superficial and trivial, reducing the specificities of individuals and organizations to accessible and calculable information, which injects a pervasive mistrust into political and psychological life. Thus have we fallen into a cycle of violence, mourning, melancholia, and revenge that shapes our everyday lives.

If the development of a counter-impulse to terror is to become more than a theoretical possibility, human beings must willingly engage in transforming the horrors of displacement by the healing gestures of compassion and forgiveness that belong to a true homecoming. For this renewal of self, earth, and world to come to fruition, we must begin to experience our displacement not only retrospectively, as the source of interminable grief, but also prospectively, as the transition that spurs human evolution toward an affective awareness of the wordless knowledge within the word. The discovery/recovery of the Divine Silence that is the eternal Source of language (*logos*)—whose sacred intimations inspire us to selflessly serve the well-being of others and the healing of the world—is the task of *modern initiation*.

Neither a revival of religious observation and symbolism nor a psycho-spiritual path to self-knowledge alone, the wordless knowledge which grounds modern initiation gives rise to an embodied awareness that all *sensory qualities* of people and things are but the outer manifestations of their inner *soul qualities*. Oriented by the heartfelt activities of reverence and surrender that support the development of new affective-cognitive faculties and incorporeal transformations, modern initiation inaugurates a *relational revolution* which allows us to overcome the intensified sense of estrangement and the aggrandizement of the ego that haunts our age, and to experience new depths of intimacy and soul-connectedness with ourselves, others, nature, and beings of the spiritual world.

If initiation is to be modern, it cannot avoid confronting the irrepressible techno-scientific management of the world. As a result of its historic embeddedness, modern initiation cannot appeal to a revival of the innocent wonder that permeated the ancient attainment of wisdom concerning life, death, and regeneration; nor can it any longer be restricted to the possession of a secret doctrine, or practiced as adherence to any prescriptive ritual. Consequently, if modern initiation is to contribute to the transition from the universalization of terror to a new beginning, it must become inspired by an *exigency to creativity*.

In its complete objectification of all aspects of social relatedness, especially its reduction of the natural world to a warehouse of disposable resources, the universalization of terror poses an immediate challenge to the creative imperative of modern initiation. In its tendency to view all questions as mere problems that are, in principle, solvable, the project of the universalization of terror is one and the same as the obliteration of the mysterious and its replacement by the sovereignty of calculation. The pervasively negative effects of this commitment to disenchantment, which include but are not limited to: cynicism concerning political change, widespread and varied addictions, disregard for ecological concerns, and the escape into virtual realities, reinforce the threat that terror's universalization will preclude historically formative actions. According to Martin Heidegger, whose thinking concerning the modern epoch has deeply influenced my understanding of terror, the more ominous danger is that existence is becoming bound up with a compulsive form of distress that compels us to forget our primordial openness to the mystery of the world. Specifically, "terror, our basic disposition,…reveals behind all progress and all domination over beings a dark emptiness and irrelevance and a shrinking back in the face of the first and last decisions" (BQ 169).

Precisely because this distress is so compelling and so secret, daring to see it for what it is provides a powerful impetus for the transition that would allow us to take distance and hold ourselves back from terror. As we rekindle the courage to detach ourselves from the abundant material and emotional enticements which consistently fail to deliver on their promise of happiness and security, we become free to appropriate our authentic selves. Abetting this process of self-discovery, the creative imperative of modern initiation cultivates our readiness to embark upon a journey which opens the soul to the living forces of the spiritual world—in which improvisation is valued over planning, surprise is always welcome, and completion cannot be envisioned in advance. I call this dangerous and opportune adventure the way to *an unknown destiny*. Modern initiation requires the embrace of a truly unknown destiny, because it is only in this unconditioned openness and detachment from preformatted determinations that we can prepare for the possibility of embodying and enacting an essentially new mode of "presencing."

The universalization of terror conditions us to believe that the material world comprises the whole of reality, and urges us to remain indifferent to its devastation of social, personal, and ecological relations; the creative imperative of modern initiation, on the other hand, inaugurates a questioning of the predetermined and prepackaged lifestyles we so uncritically accept. While the universalization of terror introduces intoxications and fascinations which compel us to want to possess what we encounter, the creative imperative of modern initiation cultivates the timid dawning of a form of attunement whereby we learn to integrate a sense of responsibility that lets what we encounter disclose itself as it is. Such attunement discloses a previously hidden rift in the world of the senses that permits the sudden shining forth of the awesome uniqueness and untranslatable singularity of beings, unencumbered by any judgment or predicate. Sheltering the disposition of awe by which the sacred illuminates us and we illuminate the sacred, the creative imperative of modern initiation allows us to come closer to the cognitive and practical faculty of *heart thinking*.

Signaling the beginning of a new stage of consciousness, heart thinking is a non-rational—but not *irrational*—mode of apprehending, by which our interactions with the world shed the egoistic character of economic exchange. Rather than focusing on the mathematical, the linear, or the logical, heart thinking takes a feeling-impression of a person or situation, registering imaginally what we usually filter out through rational consciousness, and gives this impression a creative form through poetic language. Through heart thinking we experience our impressions as evocations, invitations to meet another in a sympathetic way, and find the freedom to create a genuine and appreciative response.

In a time threatened by dehumanization and planetary destruction, the most radical virtue of heart thinking is that it brings into presence a direct, moral experience of perceiving into the world of the spirit, and translates it into an understandable linguistic-logical form. Initiated in visionary inspiration and expressible in language that is neither a human creation nor a communicative competence but whose source is instead divine, heart thinking is a transformational practice attained only through a schooling of consciousness that overcomes the materio-metaphysical presuppositions of causality that splits thought and being.

Where can this schooling of consciousness that leads to the capacity for heart thinking be learned and practiced? In the words of C. G. Jung: "The only 'initiation process' that is still alive and practiced in the West is the analysis of the unconscious...for therapeutic purposes" (1969, 514–15).

The privileged status of the psychotherapeutic encounter as an initiatory rite results from its explicit confrontation with the usually unbearable feeling of terror. As the place where we speak in free associations to embellish, intensify and modify stories of family romance, and to tell of dreams both grotesque and sublime, the psychotherapeutic encounter is doubtlessly an appropriate theater for concentration upon the mysteries and sufferings of the soul. Offering witness to those whose anxiety, depression, and humiliation betray an unconscious loss of faith, the psychotherapeutic encounter not only supports the compensatory functions of reconciliation and reparation, it also contributes to resolving the unavoidable transferences of affections that inevitably arise in therapy as well as in all intersubjective relations. By creating a place where the soul can freely and fully unfold the pain encrypted in the familial narrative and deal with the damage inflicted upon the soul by all sorts of violent abuse, psychotherapy facilitates new forms of self-expression and provides us with access to previously unavailable self-knowledge.

Yet I contend that Jung's assertion is unduly narrow. Given the all-too-easy accommodations psychotherapy has made to the adaptation strategies proposed by ego-psychology, object relations, neurobiology, self-improvement, and recovery programs, it is increasingly difficult for this process to offer guidance in how heart thinking can free us from our intrapsychic and interpersonal entrapments. Moreover, as psychology has historically aligned itself with the materialist sciences, it is increasingly rare for the psychotherapeutic encounter to esteem or promote the teaching that our personal identity exceeds the conditions of our birth and that our relatedness to others and to the world, however intimate or distant, is a manifestation of our primordial identity as given to us by the divine Other. On the other hand, by virtue of its abiding involvement in the amelioration of psychic pain and the integration of imperceptible and often unacceptable states of consciousness (whether prompted by internal conflict, relational failure, or the increasingly abstract and impersonal form of existence spawned by the universalization of terror), the psychotherapeutic encounter contributes to the dawning of a modern initiatic consciousness by enhancing awareness of the unconscious and increasing self-knowledge.

It is therefore with an eye to reorienting and expanding the role of the psychotherapeutic encounter in the dawning of a modern initiatic consciousness that I turn to the writings of Friedrich Nietzsche, Martin Heidegger, and Rudolf Steiner.

Nietzsche

Our readings of Nietzsche in the following chapters will focus on *Thus Spoke Zarathustra*, *The Antichrist*, *Ecce Homo*, and *Beyond Good and Evil*. These works not only support Stambaugh's evaluation of Nietzsche as a "poetic mystic" (1994, 135) but also illustrate that his philosophy is inseparable from his psychological observations of human nature. In advance of our readings, let us state that we will not pursue the psychological aspect of his philosophy that appears in his theory of drives, which supports his views on the will to power, nor will we emphasize his critique of religious belief, which gives rise to his doctrine of eternal recurrence. Rather, we locate the essence of Nietzsche's philosophical psychology in the prologue to *Thus Spoke Zarathustra*, where his presentation of "The Three Metamorphoses" articulates an evolutionary process of self-transformation.

Depicting an alchemical process of purification and augmentation, "The Three Metamorphoses" employs the images of the camel, the lion, and the child to symbolize Nietzsche's basic concern: the transformation of the human being after the death of God from self-alienation to the exalted freedom of an integrated self-consciousness. Showing how through self-determination we achieve autonomy and the courage to enact new values, Nietzsche's philosophical psychology elaborates a radical form of soul wisdom. As a step in the post-theological transition from man to Overman which Nietzsche proclaims to be our fate, the child represents the qualities of innocent seriousness, laughing silence, and especially improvisational play that we must embody if we are to offer moral and artistic resistance to the corrupting influences of nihilism.

It comes as no surprise that Nietzsche's subtitle for his intellectual autobiography, *Ecce Homo—How One Becomes What One Is*—is organized around the overriding task that has grown in the depths of his soul: the *revaluation of values*. Writing with the acumen of "a *psychologist* who has not his equal," Nietzsche advances his "precondition for dealing with great tasks...*play*" (EH, "Why I Write Such Good Books," #5). In fact, Nietzsche's articulation of play as a freely willed and passionate embodiment of life is not only at the heart of his new science of "joyful wisdom," it also structures his view of fate: "not merely to endure that which happens of necessity, still less to dissemble it...but to *love* it. My formula for greatness in a human being is *amor fati*" (Ibid.).

Nietzsche's affirmation of *amor fati*, love of fate, draws upon the way play stimulates artistic creativity, and is consistent with his understanding that habits of resignation and pity prevent the development of the inner strength necessary for revaluation. As a way of living that expedites the movement between overcoming and beginning, Nietzsche proposes *amor fati* as the crucial element that contributes to metamorphosis of soul. Encouraging us to face our fate with courage and grace, love motivates us to find the determination to enact our life as a fateful process. Love opens our awareness to the approaching of what is undetermined, for the coming near of the ever-present origin. Here love is truthfulness, and its transparency awakens the generosity to let the beloved be and become. Everywhere love touches the soul, the potential for transcendence blossoms and there is engendered the strange mixture of vulnerability and fearlessness that initiates the birth of another, unknown destiny. Read retrospectively, what appeared to Nietzsche as his fate alone—the revaluation of values, the creation of a new beginning of history through the transformation of the soul as a living of *amor fati*—has indeed become in this epoch of the "universalization of terror" the *destiny* of all humanity.

From the perspective of the creative imperative of modern initiation, the practice of living *amor fati* can become a path of soul-healing which both promotes awareness of spiritual wholeness, and provides the wisdom necessary for embracing the emergence of a personal destiny—the otherness of which consists in releasing us from the abjections of terror, because it is centered in the cosmic light of love.

Heidegger

The esoteric philosophy of Heidegger, whose essential focus is the question of Being (*Seinsfrage*), plays a profound role in the development of a modern initiatic consciousness. Through his idiosyncratic reading of much of the Western philosophical canon, we can appreciate the urgency of "overcoming metaphysics"; metaphysics being the condition whereby Being is reduced to and confused with beings (EP 101–10). Of crucial importance in countering the despair brought about by the universalization of terror is the essential paradox that Heidegger attempts to think through: "dwelling is the fundamental trait of the human condition" (PLT 160) and "homelessness is coming to be the destiny of the world" (LH 219).

For Heidegger, "dwelling" refers to the unconscious, pre-reflective sense of having a place in the world, which is inherent to human life. It evokes the primal sense of safety necessary for human beings to develop and mature without the fear of annihilation, such that *to dwell* amounts to the same thing as *to be*.

As analyzed by Heidegger in *Being and Time*, dwelling is threatened because human beings, which Heidegger terms *Dasein* (there/here being), are thrown into a world structured by the desires and interests of an impersonal and hierarchal collective that he refers to as "the they" (*das Man*) (BT 164). Committed to its own preservation and security, "the they" absorbs *Dasein* into everydayness and deprives it of a language (*logos*) that would give voice to the Being of dwelling, thereby insuring that the fundamental character of our relation to the spoken and the social is forgotten in what is habitual.

This forgetting entails a true crisis in dwelling and infuses us with the anxiety of homelessness—though we rarely recognize it as such. Irreducible to threats located in external causes or objects, anxiety (BT 230ff.), which both results from and contributes to a deficit of attention, further estranges us from encountering our true selves and engaging in whole, harmonious, healthy relationships. From the perspective of this existential anxiety, the crisis in dwelling reveals that it is in the very midst of everyday comfort, seemingly safe from harm and threat, that we are least attentive, thus farthest from our selves and most ill at ease.

While Heidegger speculates that the crisis in dwelling is perhaps the crisis underlying the alienation that suffuses and encompasses the modern epoch, he identifies the ground of the disaster that defines our time as the *abandonment of being* (CP 75–86). This withdrawal of Being, which coincides with the disintegration of truth and the disenchantment of nature whereby beings are deprived of their very essence, "conceals itself in the varied and increasingly widespread manifestations of *calculation, acceleration,* and the *claim of massiveness*" (Ibid., 84). The unrestrained functioning of these three forces gives evidence that we have already sub-scribed to the increasingly unquestioned belief that virtually anything we desire or imagine can be made or achieved. This belief operates through our unqualified allegiance to the domination of organized producibil-ity, which Heidegger refers to as "machination" or "technicity" (Ibid., 88–93). Driven by constantly self-surpassing progress and a need for expansion and extension that exceeds the demands of any economic sys-tem, machination or technicity strives to make beings into mere resources for its predatory will. Unrelated to any system of ethics other than its own totalization, machination suffocates being and creates a world "where self-certainty has become unsurpassable, where everything is held to be calculable and, above all, where it is decided, without a preceding question, who we are and what we are to do" (Ibid., 87). Disguising our growing emptiness and demoralization with a plethora of meaningless distractions and entertainments, machination gives rise to a form of *dis-tress* whose most shocking trait is the way it conveys a singular "*lack of distress*" (Ibid.). Fostering the appearance of self-assertion and individual freedom, machination discourages us from recognizing its constant search for unconditional power. As a "coercive force [whose] always transform-able capability for subjugation knows no discretion" (M 12), machination is an ideal handmaiden for the universalization of terror.

To counter this "will to will" that pushes toward global domina-tion, which he called "enframing" (*Gestell*) (QT), Heidegger posed, and encouraged us to pose, the question of Being. His answer to that ques-tion, which is so far from a system of norms that it often seems unintel-ligible if not unethical, is that being, in an age without a beyond, requires a certain way of life. This way of life entails unlearning the historical search for invariable standards that would ensure constant *presence*— as in the constant, goal-directed activity of total mechanization and in theological dogma—and learning a way of "releasement," or letting-be (*Gelassenheit*) (DT). A way of meditative thinking, speaking, and acting, *Gelassenheit* lets us recognize the potential for freedom in contingent, transient *events of presencing.*

Dependent upon human *Dasein* serving as the clearing of the opening that welcomes Being and safeguards its coming into unconcealment, these events are inseparable from our readiness to live a new practical understanding of dwelling. Countering, for example, the threat and deployment of mass control strategies and invasive surveillance techniques, the new practical understanding of dwelling protects the possibility of living in a truly poetic and ecophilosophical reverence for the beings and things of the earth. It is to enhance our turning toward this possibility that "releasement," or letting-be (*Gelassenheit*) prepares.

Steiner

In addition to Nietzsche's existential psychology and Heidegger's esoteric philosophy, achieving the new beginning that is the task of modern initiation requires consideration of the spiritual science of Rudolf Steiner. Although Steiner is most widely known as the founder of Waldorf education, the underlying intention of his work is the dissemination of the evolutionary meaning of the Christ Impulse (1997a; 1984). As he articulates his meditative and practical teachings for the refinement of the soul and the development of new cognitive faculties through the spiritual science of Anthroposophy, Steiner's abiding focus and inspiration is the once and unfinished event of the Mystery of Golgotha (1972; 2006).

Testifying to the continuity between the spiritual and physical-sensory worlds, the Mystery of Golgotha, which Steiner terms the pivotal event in earth and human history, signifies that a Being of a higher cosmic order entered the realm of earthly life through incarnation into the body of Jesus of Nazareth in order to participate in an element of human destiny that is unknown to the gods: the experience of birth and death. As a *supersensible* event, this sacrificial deed of the Christ allows the gods themselves to acquire inner knowledge of the mystery of birth and of death as it can only be experienced on the earth by human beings. As an *earthly* event for human beings, whose loss of comprehension of the primeval wisdoms coincides with our descent into materialism, the death and resurrection of Christ *and* His ongoing participation in evolution reveal to us the divine and eternal nature of our own souls.

Building upon these and other understandings of the Mystery of Golgotha, Steiner seeks to prepare us for the reappearance or *second coming* of Christ, albeit in the nonphysical form of an angel, which he sees occurring during and beyond the twentieth century (1983a). Aware that both creative and destructive spiritual forces are at play in the cosmic-earthly event of the second coming, and that these forces have both direct and indirect influences on our receptivity to Christ, Steiner gave constant attention to the problem of evil. His path of attaining spiritual knowledge, achieved especially through meditative practices that emphasize the soul quality of selflessness and the developmental capacity for heart thinking, not only serves as a counter to the universalization of terror, but also unfolds a form of initiation that is appropriate for the consciousness of modern souls.

In late September of 1923, Steiner visited Vienna for the last time. As part of a short lecture series, *Michaelmas and the Soul-Forces of Man*, he gave a talk entitled "Michael, the Dragon, and the Human Soul or *Gemut*" in which he shared his vision for the development of new capacities for affective-cognitions that can resist the expanding range of evil. Rearticulating the cosmic image of the Archangel Michael slaying the Dragon, Steiner's approach to the cosmic image is not a repetition of ancient mythology, but a way for occult teaching to offer knowledge appropriate for initiating a modern and postmodern consciousness of spiritual realities and beings. Postulating that the "last third of the nineteenth century stands for something extraordinarily important for human evolution" (1994b, 212), Steiner questions whether human beings can respond to the "death of God" otherwise than by falling prey to new forms of fanaticism, (among which he counts psychoanalysis). Aware that our answer to this question discloses whether we are prepared to actualize freedom in the service of love, the only path capable of overcoming the dual evils of egoism and materialism, Steiner attempts to mobilize the coalescence of soul-spiritual forces so that slaying the Dragon becomes an inner experience. Bypassing the Freudian approach, which remains embedded in the morass of sexual causality and repressed subconscious forces from which it wishes to escape, he concludes his talk with the following spiritual meditation:

> The power of the Dragon is working within me, trying to drag me down. I do not see it. I *feel* it as something that would drag me down beneath myself. But in the spirit I *see* the luminous Angel whose cosmic task has always been the vanquishing of the Dragon. I concentrate my soul upon this glowing figure, I let its light stream into my *Gemut,* and thus my soul, illumined and warmed, will bear within the strength of Michael. Hence, out of my own freedom, I shall be able, through my alliance with Michael, to conquer the might of the Dragon in my lower nature. (Ibid.)

Rather than guiding us through an intellectual analysis of the feelings associated with the internal workings of the Dragon, Steiner is interested in helping us to open our souls to freely assume responsibility for overcoming the evil impulses that are lodged in the subconscious. Consequently, he offers this meditation as a way to form a spiritual alliance with the presence of the Angel. In addition to its pedagogic and therapeutic value, the meditation becomes the path upon which there can arise the experiences of cognitive expansion and incorporeal transmutation necessary for creating the new postmodern structure of spiritual awareness. By redirecting toward the spiritual world the battle against the evils that have descended upon us coincident with the belief in the "death of God," Steiner informs us that human existence is simultaneously earthly and cosmic. More importantly, he prepares us to meet the pivotal transformative event that he sees occurring throughout and beyond the twentieth century with both faith and love: the reappearance of Christ in the etheric (i.e., the non-physical reality that surrounds and infuses physical bodies) (1983a, 69–89).

In addition to helping us attain etheric vision, Rudolf Steiner designed his meditations to secure our release from imprisonment in the bewildering contradictoriness and dualities of the interior psyche that materialist psychology promulgates by defining psyche in isolation from the world. He was aware not only of the doubt, hostility, and resignation produced by this isolation, but also of the paralyzing fear that could arise with the psyche's perception of what has been ordinarily inconceivable and normally invisible.

It is hardly surprising that tales of spiritual perception should come to expression in the psychotherapeutic encounter. Given that these soul narratives reflect a mutation in consciousness that seeks to communicate unformulated experiences containing bizarre objects and spiritual subjects, how will psychotherapists who are trained to reject spiritual realities and beings interpret them? Will psychotherapists become unduly alarmed when their patients' initial efforts at inspired self-transformation appear escapist and immature, give evidence of schizoid-like symptoms, or even enact psychotic-like behaviors? Will psychotherapists judge these soul expansions as aberrant and take recourse in the rigidity of pathological diagnoses and/or resort to premature medication? Or will they surmount their own limiting preconceptions and welcome these new experiential displacements toward the "numinous" as occasions to openly face the transcendent play of the sacred?

Steiner's teachings concerning the beginning of spirit perception change the entire context for the therapeutic work of soul maturation and transformation. The metamorphoses of soul necessary for transformation in our epoch render the analysis of resistance and interpretation of symbols, however crucial to the process of individuation, inadequate. Instead of promoting the goals of recollection, attaining personal empowerment, or elaborating strategies of behavioral modification, which are merely props to shore up the unstable esteem of a self that remains ignorant of its own nature, Steiner's *psychosophy* is oriented to the realization of moral attitudes that are truly creative, such as wonder, reverence, and devotion; and to awakening our apprehension of a "time current coming from the future" (1990, 135). In addition to disclosing that our essential soul-being is animated by spiritual forces that can free us from entrapment in matter, Steiner's teachings propose an answer to the challenge posed by the call of an unknown destiny: *to reverse the incarnational path taken by the evil spirits and engage in an ascensional migration.*

Through the free raising of our consciousness that Steiner opens to us as a possibility, including awareness of reincarnation and karma (1992), Anthroposophy

> should be remolded in our souls into capacities for qualitatively higher human feeling (*Gemut*) and character, into an entirely different mood of soul orientation, disposition of mind, faculty of perception (*Gesinnung*), and … should make totally different human beings of us. (1983a, lecture of January 25, 1910)

It is by nurturing and welcoming this deepening of the soul that initiation can fulfill its calling and enable human beings to find the hope and courage necessary for spiritual transformation.

* * *

In the work of Nietzsche, Heidegger, and Steiner, one can discern a conversation that did and did not happen. Though these thinkers never collaborated in their work, it is as if they spoke to each other obliquely in conceiving their own authentic responses to the same fearsome threat.

In order to understand this phenomenon, the universalization of terror, which has continued to gain strength since its emergence at the beginning of the twentieth century, I believe we must engage with Nietzsche, Heidegger, and Steiner today. As all three observed and deeply feared the loss of human potentials for creativity, freedom, and transcendence, all three also strove earnestly to uphold them in ever new and living ways. If forms of liberation from this all-encompassing terror are to be found and given shape, these thinkers offer the profoundest meditations on routes of escape. Yet it is not only evasion they offer us, but questings toward an unknown destination, whereby affirmation of life, the mode of being that most defines the truly human, initiates the self-transcendence that unfolds through commitment and openness to the power of pure possibility.

Chapter 1

FROM ORNITHOLOGY TO A LOVE SUPREME: OVERCOMING THE FORCES OF GRAVITY, AND THE TEACHING OF *AMOR FATI*

I T IS A STRANGE and unsettling experience to come upon the self-proclaimed teacher of the "transvaluation of values" through the healing joy of *amor fati* overwhelmed by enmity. Yet this is the disposition of Nietzsche's Zarathustra in the teaching of *Thus Spoke Zarathustra* that concerns us: "Of the Spirit of Gravity" (210–13). Assuming that enmity has no place in the transcendent possibilities Nietzsche proclaims, we would not expect to be greeted by a hostile prophet. Confronted with Zarathustra's uncompromising and consuming hatred, we might at first wonder whether his sullen brooding reflects an "antisocial personality disorder."

On the other hand, imagining the performative rather than the pathological perspective to be operative, we could study the antagonism oozing from Zarathustra as an indicator of the conflict that awaits human beings in their contemporary knowledge quest: one that necessitates overcoming what Nietzsche calls the Spirit of Gravity.

The Spirit of Gravity orients the basic universal forces of weight and significance in a fixed and immutable downward direction. The Spirit of Gravity also refers to a psychological complex that entails certain symptomatic attributes and attitudes that Nietzsche finds antagonistic to the transcendent powers of life, and anathema to Eternal Return, the book's "central fable" (Lampert 1986), through which he asks, "Can I affirm living my life over and over again just as it is for all eternity?"

To fulfill his chosen role as the one who proclaims the coming of the Overman (*Übermensch*)—the transitional creative figure who emerges after the death of God—Zarathustra must show his listeners how the "gravitization" of all aspects of everyday life both encroaches upon our freedom and forecloses the possibilities for "transvaluation." By disclosing how Gravity sustains the habitual mental impressions left by older systems of philosophy, such as Platonism, asceticism, and stoicism, and inculcates oppressive inhibitions that exclusively venerate patterns of emotional severity, sobriety, and stability, Nietzsche hopes to commence a reorientation of evaluating that highlights the interconnected wholeness of the self-other-world matrix. Under the conditions of indeterminacy that mark this reorientation, the boundaries necessary to maintain the familiar space-time continuum do not disappear, but become light enough to be moved. In addition, by advocating contemplative and playful immersion in the preciousness and fragility of the moment, Zarathustra opens a path of "self-surpassing" that rests upon our awareness that we are co-creators of our personal-social reality—that its values are easily invertible and its perspectives reversible.

While Zarathustra affirms that he "can and *will*" contest the seemingly inescapable force of Gravity ("I am the enemy to the Spirit of Gravity: and truly, mortal enemy, arch-enemy, born enemy!"), he feels this enmity impedes his teaching. As a remedy for the malady of Gravity, he shuns the talking cure; instead he prescribes silent retreats in a "home" whose isolation and emptiness are the opposite of familiarity and comfort. Zarathustra's retreats, however, do not signify escapism, dissociation, or a fall into despair. Rather, they are freely chosen opportunities to engage in *meditation* (which for him focuses especially upon "ornithological" themes and images of a "birdlike" nature). In fact, these meditation retreats are forays into an ideal or contemplative atmosphere that deepens Zarathustra's self-resolve and furthers his intention to provide healing and hope.

Given the modern epoch's obsession with the active domination of the external world, especially through techno-scientific means, it is hardly surprising that Zarathustra's organizing idea and art, Eternal Return, has been met with great animus. Negative assessments of Nietzsche's health and philosophy extend even to C. G. Jung, who spent the five years between 1934 and 1939 giving private seminars in Zurich on *Zarathustra* (1988). In particular, Jung's antagonism toward the affirmation of Eternal Return, given his own therapeutic commitment to the psychic elaboration of mythic symbols and his discovery of the collective unconscious, is surprising. Most critically, and perhaps acting on the contempt bred of familiarity, Jung undervalues the way the drama enacted in *Zarathustra* demonstrates the process of "internalization through sacrifice" that he himself advances for achieving both therapeutic resolution of the transference and a life devoted to creative individuation (CW, vol. 16).

Indeed, the aphoristic and enigmatic composition of *Zarathustra*, which Nietzsche declares is both "descriptual and destinal" (1979, 69–82), eludes easy understanding. Specifically, we regard its intentional disruptions of ordinary modes of thinking, feeling, and willing as requiring a reading that performs multiple, differential interpretations. From this heterogeneous approach, we must reject Jung's interpretation of the relationship between Nietzsche and the figure of Zarathustra as a symptom of pathological fusion. On the contrary, we read this complex relationship as the inception of a philosophical psychology whose purpose is to generate a desire for the experience of initiation.

To substantiate the claim that initiatic experience is both the source and the aim of Nietzsche's endeavor of philosophical psychology, we will again refer to his textual autobiography, *Ecce Homo* (94–112). Writing with an intensity that reflects the hurt of non-recognition, Nietzsche laments that he has never been asked what the figure of Zarathustra means to *him*. In answer to the unasked question, Nietzsche offers a concise description of a genealogy of morals. He then unambiguously proclaims that his work is permeated with evaluations infused by the "Persian" influence. Yet Nietzsche expects that ignorance and/or distortion of ancient Persian wisdom will spawn misunderstandings of his work into the future. We might even imagine his extremely personal answer to the Zarathustra question to be accompanied by the following warning to his readers:

Zarathustra's teachings contain eternal mystical truths. Failure to confront these teachings with meditative reading and compassionate living will contribute to the destruction of entire cultures.

Especially in the modern epoch, ignorance of Zarathustran initiatic theory and practice will accelerate the fall into nihilism and the emergence of an essential immorality riddled with the instinct for revenge.

Heeding this implicit warning, we will follow his directions and attempt to understand *Zarathustra* as "Persian" (and, indeed, to determine just what that may mean). Undertaking this attempt, we accept Nietzsche's invitation to become one of his readers of the future. At the same time, in creating our own interpretations we will choose to "stand apart" from him—for his plea authorizes us to author our own reading of the future. In this way our reading of *Zarathustra* will attempt three ventures:

To identify and preserve the enduring value of *truthfulness* characteristic of the Persian Wisdom Teacher.

To thus discern Nietzsche's call for us to engage with and enact moral wisdom.

To welcome the arrival of this call at the beginning of the twenty-first century as an awakening of a commitment to countering Gravity in its manifestations of nihilism and terror.

Persian Flights

We will begin our reading of *Zarathustra* by observing how its Prologue introduces the biographical situation of Zarathustra:

When Zarathustra was thirty years old, he left his home and the lake of his home and went into the mountains. Here he had the enjoyment of his spirit and his solitude and did not weary of it for ten years. But at last his heart turned...

Zarathustra's ten-year meditation with the Solar Spirit comes to completion not with the passage of any examination, but with a transformation of his heart. It bears mentioning here that Zarathustra originally sought wisdom after a singularly painful heartbreak. As told in Schuré's occult history (1982), the spiritual biography of Asjabr (Zarathustra's tribal name) begins when his violent enemies, the Turanians, enslave Ardouizur, an uncommonly beautiful and proud woman of his race. Humiliated by his failure to secure her freedom by substituting his own subjugation for hers, Asjabr grieves as if for a lost love. Refusing to be condemned to powerlessness, and consumed by the thirst for truth and revenge, Asjabr comes to study with Vahumanu, the last descendant of the priests of the Spiritual Sun. Eventually renouncing his position in the world, Asjabr becomes the initiate Zarathustra ("shining or dancing star"), apostle of Ahura-Mazda (the great wisdom-filled Spirit, the great aura). The disciple Zarathustra's twofold mission consists of physically and intellectually overcoming the negative powers of the Turanians and leading the evolution of consciousness by educating human beings in the arts of agriculture and the earth sciences.

Against this cosmo-mythic background, we can imagine that Zarathustra's initiation included exposure to devouring animal forces and demonic temptations; we can also expect that an initiation of this intensity has included a near-death and rebirth experience. These rites enhance Zarathustra's faithful and ardent quest for morality and truth-fulness. Furthermore, they develop new inner qualities of reverence, patience, and intuitive knowledge which prompt him to ask the right questions and take the right actions. As a consequence of these transfor-mations, Zarathustra is awakened by Ahura-Mazda to the reality of the spiritual being of Darkness, Ahriman.

Working from the center of the earth and directly into the bodies and minds of human beings, Ahriman seeks dominion of the planet by drawing souls toward the world of matter and away from the world of spirit. Ahriman deploys various downward-pulling forces to afflict souls with a virulent tendency to fall away from truth and life and become preoccupied instead with illusion and death. Confronted by this gravi-tational power in which truth is identical to the pragmatic workings of material power, Zarathustra is challenged to translate the language of metaphysics into the realm of morality. Not satisfied simply to demon-strate that "the struggle between good and evil is the actual wheel in the working of things" (EH 97–98), Zarathustra is determined to teach souls how they themselves can manifest the reality of moral goodness in the world.

Zarathustra knows well that Ahriman pulls the soul exclusively toward the illusory solidity of the perishable earth. As a particularly strong impediment to our continuity of consciousness upon entering the spiritual world, Ahriman implants in us an attitude toward life that comes to expression in the instinct for revenge: claiming the material world as our only home, we demand payback for the wrongs we suffer, for where else can these wrongs be redressed? From the prior collapse of his own will, Zarathustra is aware that this desire for payback engenders the attitude of *ressentiment*, which is often expressed in the compulsive acting out of vengeance and the obsessive wish that the world were otherwise. To counter this reactionary tendency in the human soul, Zarathustra provides practical-moral teachings that enable us to elude Ahriman's intention to preoccupy us with the precariousness of material survival. As we come to appreciate Nietzsche's understanding of Persian initiation in its psycho-moral and political aspects, we also recognize that Zarathustra is a representative of the spiritual archetype whose teachings concern the way souls can manage the conflict between violence and peace which faces all temporal beings, for all time.

Attaining awareness of this trans-temporal and cultural-ethical perspective, we can posit that the enmity that opens Zarathustra's encounter with the Spirit of Gravity is not a symptom of manic-depressive possession. Rather, his disturbance is an aftereffect of the aspect of initiation wherein his will is awakened for deeds he must undertake against Ahriman. From this observation, I contend that Zarathustra's dis-ease is a transitional form of the passionate moral conviction whose unleashing moves his teaching to challenge all the dogmatisms sponsored by Gravity. The animosity evident in this "unavoidable psychologist and reader of souls, who *needs* hardness and cheerfulness more than other men," (BGE #269) is a liminal condition resulting from a spiritual initiation intended to overcome all that is petty and vulgar in the soul.

Accepting Nietzsche's description, we intuit that Zarathustra's initiation includes the relaxation of connections to the physical body as well as the establishment of a cognitive correspondence between macrocosmic and microcosmic wisdoms. Achieving this sophianic conjunction without eliminating the differences between the sense and spiritual worlds, Zarathustra unfolds teachings that instruct the soul on becoming flexible enough to speak against all fatalisms while remaining morally steadfast and nonjudgmental. We also notice that his post-initiatic speaking takes the form of singing protest songs. And given that the word *song* appears in the title of seven of Zarathustra's teachings, (night, dance, funeral, second dance, seals of Yes and Amen, melancholy, and intoxication), it behooves us to observe not only how music gives form to his curative therapy, but that artistic creativity is the impetus that advances both the moral development of the soul and a more integrated human relationship between earth and cosmos.

Turning directly to the chapter "Of the Spirit of Gravity," we find Zarathustra describing the future condition of human beings whose initiation has been accompanied by a music that he later calls ecstatic:

He who will one day teach men to fly will have moved all boundary-stones; all boundary-stones will themselves fly into the air to him, he will baptize the earth anew—as "the weight-less."

In such flight, perhaps, is founded Jung's criticism that Zarathustra's teaching "leads into the complete annihilation of law and order, and of nature as well, the nature that is heavy and has definite landmarks... upset[ting] the natural order of things, creating beings who have no soil under their feet" (1988, 1470). To understand why Zarathustra personifies the future earth teacher as an "ecstatic" who is capable of overcoming the laws of nature, we must diverge from Jung and willingly enter the "labyrinth of daring knowledge." To help us accomplish this rite of passage, we will assume the figure of Zarathustra's "perfect reader": a "monster of courage and curiosity, also supple, cunning, cautious, a born adventurer and discoverer" (EH 43). Attempting to approximate this challenging ideal, we listen to the rapturous music of the Persian's teaching and understand the moods it evokes as clues on the path to creative self-transcendence.

Jung's admonishment of Nietzsche for transmitting an idea that denies the inviolable laws of the earth and endangers groundedness reflects a lack of receptivity to Zarathustra's teaching of ecstatic flight. Unbinding the personality from encapsulation in egoic consciousness, ecstatic flight or levitation is in this case not a symptom of arrogant inflation, but an initiatory practice engaged in by the soul to prepare it for the appearance of an archetypal and inspirational cosmic being. Furthermore, we sense that Zarathustra's vision song offers "soil" for those who seek to grow beyond the identification of home, self, and other with the sclerotic and ultimately deathbound processes of mineralization. We read of transcending gravity not as an example of hallucination, nor as an aesthetic-political project that anticipates surrealism, but as affirming the possibility of metamorphic or creative transfiguration. Refusing promises of otherworldly bliss, Zarathustra's teaching of ecstatic flight invites the soul to activate elevations in consciousness that invoke the possibility that the earth can become a planetary sphere of *lightness*.

Zarathustra begins the "ornithological" aspect of his teaching by offering a comparative picture between the art of flight and the "logic of the ostrich." Zarathustra does not demean the ostrich, which when frightened can only react according to the instinct for preservation and stick its head in the earth. He is, however, impatient with human beings who indulge in self-deception and refuse to confront their fears from the heights of truth. Intimating that we have become our own worst enemies by filling our thinking with doubt and our feeling with the tendency to blame, Zarathustra offers flight as a response to the conflict with gravity. Elevating us to a position of stillness from which we can enliven the health of our knowledge, Zarathustra teaches flight as a gesture of retreat rather than an abandonment of the contest. A conscious invocation of an injunctive/transgressive contradiction, Zarathustran flight defers the eventuality of decision that would determine the evolution of a new system of transit. Moreover, since Zarathustra's flight is always a return flight, always a return to further encounters with the oppressive forces of Gravity, its (re)turnings depend upon whether thinking can attain a new sense of enthusiasm and a new route of expression.

Combating Gravity, Zarathustra is a joyous destroyer. He is not, however, a passive nihilist who despairs over the collapse of values that have been revealed to be untenable. Rather, his aim is to enhance moral life by displacing traditional and inherited systems of belief, thus allowing us to perceive that much of what we claim as our identity is also the source of our suffering. Thus, when Zarathustra "flies" toward the new horizon of the "boundaryless," his intent is not to avoid human embodiment and responsibility, but to loosen the identifications that are attached to the conviction that the "earth and life are heavy." Having meditatively incorporated the majesty and mobility symbolized by his omnipresent and loyal eagle, Zarathustra clarifies how Gravity obscures sight, impedes realization of celestial knowledge, and retards the solidifying of moral conscience that could bring justice and healing to social institutions which have become petrified.

From these considerations of the art of flight in Zarathustra's initiation, and recognizing that his lofty aim is a transvaluation of the moral values that bind human souls to the processes of the earth, let us elaborate the esoteric practice that supports his elevation of consciousness: the Bird-Flight meditation.

Meditation

The Bird-Flight meditation that we see embedded in Zarathustra's teaching is nowhere explicated in the text. Yet we may intuit that its presence derives from the diverse yogas of the Vedic tradition, all of which emphasize specific breath practices and body postures for the realization of states and stages of *union*. Teaching flight as a path to purify the physical body and liberate the soul, Zarathustra seeks not to *escape* illness, emotional suffering, and death, but to encourage *transcendence*. To illuminate this process of creative surpassing, which necessitates the difficult effort of impulse control and the cognitive expansion of the soul by the inflowing of spiritual ideas, Zarathustra sets the Bird-Flight meditation against the celestial horizon symbolized by the azure sky.

As the unchanging meditative background against which thinking can empty itself of preconceptions, the sky's pure blue serves to enhance concentration. As the non-obtrusive horizon against which the practitioner projects the clouds of obscurity, fear, and pain, this sky provides a clear canvas for unbiased observation of the comings and goings of sense-based consciousness. Becoming absorbed into the sky's enduring openness to the point of surrender, the meditator gains the ability to acknowledge thought patterns and behavioral structures without attracting or distributing any emotional accretion. As this skill of non-reactive noticing deepens, the practitioner begins to experience a softening of these previously consolidated states and an awareness of their essential impermanence.

Achieving perception of the invisible forces that give form to manifest thought-feelings, the practitioner of Zarathustra's Bird-Flight meditation begins to develop the capacity for *imaginal* perception. Signaling attainment of an intensified meditative integrity, imaginal perception is associated with the opening of insight. According to the researches of Georges Bataille, the inner experience of imaginal perception gives rise to a pressure at the summit of the skull that activates the "pineal eye, which, detaching itself from the horizontal system of ocular vision, appears in a kind of nimbus of tears, like the eye of a tree or, perhaps, like a human tree" (1985, 84). Awakened to this state of imaginal perception, where "the eye is without a doubt the symbol of the dazzling sun" (Ibid., 74), the meditator becomes suffused with a warmth-light that rhythmically circulates throughout and around the physical body. As the practitioner experiences this new imaginal breathing process to the point where consciousness is heightened beyond the limits of sense perception, there arises the possibility of "discharges of energy at the top of the head" (Ibid., 75). According to Bataille's anti-scientific mythological anthropology, the vertical displacement of the "eruptive/ expulsive" function from the "root chakra region" to the enclosed pineal eye facilitates face-to-face contemplation of the sun. Alongside this evolutionary development, attainment of this contemplative state facilitates the practitioner's experience of "identification... where, after a long period of servility, human beings would have an eye just for the sun" (Ibid., 74). As a consequence of the arising of imaginal perception, the opening of the previously virtual pineal eye and its transformation into a celestial eye illuminates to the practitioner the sovereignty of a cosmic sun that irradiates finite material existence with spiritual realities.

The realization of relationships permeated by soul-spiritual forces and solar wisdom demands that our further interpretation of Gravity discern and evoke the psychological and artistic attributes necessary for us to become slayers of the "slave morality" that Nietzsche associates with nihilism. Energetically, nihilism gravitates toward fatalism and heaviness, leaving the physical body in a state of chronic fatigue that demands constant recharging. Psychologically, nihilism exacerbates the attitudes of cynicism and aloofness that induce acquiescence to the destructive oscillation between personal isolation and addictive codependencies. In addition to creating emotional impoverishment, expressed in mood swings that range from uncaring indifference to violent fanaticism, nihilism is also inseparable from economic impoverishment, exploiting natural resources, and corrupting the quality of human work.

In response, Nietzsche offers a critique of nihilism based on a teaching of self-overcoming that affirms the increased power of the spirit and the peaceful and healing effects of inner lightness. Specifically, he encourages us to disconnect the soul from its attachments to the perniciousness of revenge so that we can engage in processes of maturation and refinement, making his transformative teaching synonymous with the process of continuous enlightenment. Naming the type of soul he envisions as a practitioner of his philosophical psychology, Nietzsche calls the initiate *Overman* (*Übermensch*).

The most pronounced characteristic of Nietzsche's Overman is a strengthened will to power. If the Overman is to act as a counter force to nihilism, however, this strengthened will must be directed away from purposes of domination and toward practices that demonstrate self-reflexivity and self-resistance. Contributing to a conscious and philosophical awareness of how the empowered will can refrain from acting in self-aggrandizing ways, the Bird-Flight meditation teaches a mode of strengthening that promises more than the power to manipulate or control; it realizes beauty and singularity. Viewed from this aesthetic-moral perspective, the Overman is not an ideal human being of the future, but a figure of eternal transcendence; one who, standing "beyond good and evil," expresses Nietzsche's vision of affective-cognitive enlightenment. He is the soul whose spiritual initiation entails learning to live in the affirmation, and even celebration, of pain and paradox. As such, the Overman cultivates and beautifies the self and its relationship to the world and cosmos through willing deeds that embody empathic attunement and express an uncompromising interest in social justice. In our post-Nietzschean era, the Bird-Flight meditation may proceed through visual imagery therapy, "holotropic breathing" (Grof 1988), and/or with the ingestion of entheogenic or sacred plants (McKenna 1992). What is of consequence here is not the method but the imperative of the Bird-Flight meditation. By enabling the Overman to ascend beyond the emotional and material enmeshments that habitually trap consciousness between devitalizing self-recrimination and the externalization of violence, the meditation contributes to our souls' becoming permeated by a *"sound and healthy love."*

On the Way to Love

To understand how Zarathustra's teaching of a *"sound and healthy love"* acts as an antidote to Gravity, we must begin by stipulating that this form of love, even though it is characterized as a "love of oneself," is not to be confused with narcissistic self-love (itself an attribute of Gravity). Zarathustra attempts to establish this difference by announcing that love is something human beings must *learn*. In the absence of this learning, he warns, Gravity works to press out our instincts of attraction and repulsion into prefabricated structures of meaning where narcissism flourishes and our relationships, both private and public, are susceptible to banality and fetishism. In his opposition to this pacification and perversion of soul, wherein we become easy prey to feelings of victimization and self-pity, Zarathustra is determined to help us learn how to appreciate the moment of optimum aliveness so that we can *live* life rather than *endure* it.

From his own sufferings, Zarathustra is only too aware that Gravity contributes to the annihilation of love by instituting a repetitiveness which diminishes our capacity for enchantment. Rejecting the unconscious tendency whereby the soul deliberately places itself in distressing situations that repeat an old experience without allowing its prototype to be recalled, Zarathustra's teaching counters the insufferable drone that "life is hard to bear" by invoking the challenge of personal responsibility. In asserting that "only man is hard to bear," Zarathustra denies souls the path of rationalization that would meet the difficulties of life by indulging in defeatist excuses or defensive explanations; or by sacrificing our valuable life forces to the "lying and dissembling of Gravity." Thus, while Zarathustra experiences a profound sadness that life for many has become nothing but the burden of carrying "too many *foreign* heavy words and values," his teaching never ceases to affirm the creative aspect of the will, especially as it pertains to learning the moral significance of love. Always in flight from the onerousness of existence emptied of joy, Zarathustra prefers instead to cultivate the "finest, subtlest, ultimate and most patient" of the moral arts, for he knows that these qualities ramify and diversify love.

An important aspect of Zarathustra's overcoming of Gravity includes employing the practices of lightness to "silence the mole and the dwarf." In order to quiet these antagonizing representatives of Gravity, whose deformities never let us forget the processes of degeneration that characterize the physical body, Zarathustra endeavors to transform the alienation that invariably results when expressions of affection serve to disguise the workings of self-love. Against the erotic seductions and neurotic enticements promulgated by these earthbound symbols of deceptiveness and greed, I suggest that Zarathustra's teaching of a "love of oneself" promotes a relational intimacy characterized by amorous discourse and selfless devotion. As an arousal of reciprocal expressions of heartfelt honesty and mutual respect, Zarathustran intimacy aims toward at a union of love and life in the attitude of soul which Nietzsche associates with *nobility*.

Nietzsche asks, as we might well ask today, "What is Noble?" To take up this question thoughtfully requires that we acknowledge the way our reality principle is determined by the priorities of the technosciences. In the telemedia and the network culture it spawns, the idea of nobility is lost amid the celebration of vanity and the vanities of celebrities. We have retained a sense of elitism, based on the appearances that sustain the cult of fame and wealth, but have lost the qualities that once animated the soul to fulfill its transcendent possibilities and purpose.

As a remedy for the nihilist puncturing of the hierarchic, "vertical" dimension associated with nobility, Nietzsche emphasizes an "*instinct for rank* which is more than anything else already the sign of a high rank" (BGE #263). True "rank," according to Nietzsche, relies upon the soul's attaining "some fundamental certainty regarding itself," manifesting as the generosity, trust, and trustworthiness that *nobility* implies. This quality "may not be sought or found, and perhaps may not be lost either" (BGE #287); it is a mysterious something that belongs to the soul, but is not its possession. Nietzsche offers us the cryptic image of "a *delight* in the nuances of reverence" (BGE #263)—nuances we can perceive today whenever relationships between souls and relationships with the soul of the world come to presence in the light of pure, unimpeded awareness. More precisely, when the conduct of relationships becomes a spiritual path for us to facilitate the potential for undistorted communication and the extension of unconditional hospitality toward our neighbors, soul life can become a living union between wisdom and love.

Perhaps counterintuitively, Nietzsche's rethinking of nobility requires the full exposure by the ego of its most inferior thoughts, insecure feelings, and disavowed passions to the light of pure awareness. From an understanding of the cultivation of nobility as part of a contemporary path of soul initiation, it is hardly surprising that the Overman engages in conscious journeys to inner depths that are commanded by energies and images of the grotesque. Indeed, it appears that Nietzsche's rehabilitation of the word *noble* applies most directly to those souls whose quest for self-ascendant knowledge requires a fierce and frightening *descent*. For a soul to meet the uncompromising demands of this requirement, Zarathustra suggests cultivating what he calls "taste."

Zarathustra's "taste" is not only an aesthetic sophistication but a moral maturity that arises out of one's own lived experience, and for which one takes personal responsibility. Developing taste as a way of moral perception therefore necessitates that the soul break with habits of behavior that rely on self-preservation, especially those which take recourse in blaming others and in finding "causes" for present situations in past conditions. Since this transformation in self-organization is marked by a new vulnerability and despair, Zarathustra realizes that it is almost impossible for most souls to acquire the taste for moral perception without a thorough curative education. As we have noticed, a crucial aspect of this schooling of consciousness, in which the learning of a "love of oneself" is the precondition for clarifying the grounds of our own responsibility, is the development of the "taste" for reverence. Only the refinement of this soul quality, where the capacity for veneration becomes the way that light and lightness guide the cultivation and living of sound and healthy relationships, and informs a public discourse that would renew social and political life, allows Nietzsche's Overman, as well as all souls on the path of initiation, to become masters in the "*art of style*" (EH 44).

Nietzsche's advocacy of a "style" that is noble in taste obviously has nothing to do with accumulating the objects of antiquity or memorizing arcane philosophies. Neither does his esteem for "style" reflect any encouragement for exhibitionism and grandiosity. On the other hand, "style" is seen and lived everywhere by noble souls whose capacity for unimpeded awareness and reverence allows living relationships to unfold in the *pathos of distance* (BGE #257). Relationships that live in this space, which is simultaneously open and focused, concentrated but not fused, reveal both the appreciation of beauty and the respect for truthfulness. Imploring the noble soul to fashion the self as an artist's instrument which impeccably embodies the "tempo and gesture" that frees the will for moral deeds, Nietzsche beckons those who would become initiates to embark upon journeys of aimless wandering and to experiment with different forms of thinking and affective life. This practice of abandoning the comforts of the familiar and of crossing borders between time zones, cultural communities, and modes of conceptualization enables the seeker to develop a metaperspective on human experiences and types that is an impossibility for "he who whitewashes his house." Preferring the colors of "deep yellow and burning red," which symbolize the taste for creative combat, Zarathustra urges us to transform our existence—rather than endure the grim heaviness of Gravity, to dare to develop unimpeded awareness and to begin the task of imagining and embodying the future, continually.

Cautioning that one "cannot learn to fly by flying," Zarathustra tells us that he has become who he is through traveling "diverse paths and ways": meditation, healing, prophecy, and above all, "walking among the shop-keepers and the kings." He also admits of the temptation during his "attempting and questioning" to ask the Truth of the Way. Zarathustra confesses, however, that he never subordinated his mission to overcome Gravity and that he inquired of other teachers "unwillingly," for "one has to *learn* how to answer such questioning" for oneself.

Channeling Zarathustra's hard-earned wisdom, Nietzsche's psycho-philosophical comprehension of contemporary nihilism, wherein Gravity clothes itself in unprecedented forms of terror, leads him to search for souls unafraid to become creators of their own moral values. Nietzsche's assimilation of the teaching of a "love of oneself" consists of, but is not limited to, the qualitative images that Zarathustra gives of the Overman, especially his vigorous ardor for awakening the will. Indeed, all of Zarathustra's moral-practical meditations for cultivating nobility of soul bring us closer to the ideal of the Overman. Especially as they relate to living relationships in pure awareness, they satisfy Nietzsche's "formula for greatness in a human being," *amor fati*:

> That one wants nothing to be other than it is, not in the future, not in the past, not in all eternity. Not merely to endure what happens of necessity, still less to dissemble it—all idealism is untruthfulness in the face of necessity—but to *love* it... (EH 37–38)

Amor Fati

Nietzsche's affirmation of *amor fati*, love of fate, which I interpret as his rearticulation of Zarathustra's teaching of a "love of oneself," requires that we reject the idea of fate as a fixed and unalterable orientation of events moving toward a necessary outcome, or the promise and eventual achievement of a final state. Additionally, and perhaps more importantly, given Nietzsche's observation of the historical and psychological loss of reference to an externally deterministic authority (whether biological, political, or theological), his affirmation of *amor fati* is both the logical consequence of, and a passionate response to, the death of God. The connection between these aspects of *amor fati* necessitates coming to terms with the reality that the world we inhabit is in a state of incessant and eternal becoming. Radically imminent and indeterminate, the unfinished and always-beginning quality of becoming that lies at the core of *amor fati* suggests a new experience of fate. Rather than being permeated by resignation, this new experience of fate suggests the intertwining of necessity and freedom.

Once we have been liberated from the behavioral and ethical restrictions imposed by religious doctrine, and released from the compulsion to believe in some initial or final cause and meaning, our fate becomes inseparable from the freedom to exercise world-forming powers. Most profoundly, we manifest this freedom by embracing the world that is as it is rather than in how it "should" be; for, given the world's transitory and goalless immediacy, there is no longer any "should" that can act as a judgment of deficiency. In a world where values are fleeting and the refinement of the noble soul has no significance, Nietzsche's advocacy of *amor fati* as a way to overcome the Spirit of Gravity serves as a critique of passive—or active—acceptance of hierarchy. Well aware that countering the seemingly immutable force of Gravity means undertaking an unflinchingly honest and thorough examination of our basic assumptions about social and psychic reality, Nietzsche insists that living *amor fati* will require the complete dissolution of our ingrained feelings of helplessness and unworthiness. For this transformative process to bear the psycho-spiritual fruit that can nourish the soul's self-reliance and goodness, it is necessary that we freely choose as our guide to becoming the comprehensive and inventive power of creativity.

Most people know, if only at a subconscious level, that creativity is basically synonymous with love. Consequently, living *amor fati* challenges the soul who would become ennobled to creatively disassemble its usual space-time focus and to enter alternative paths of experience. By appealing to and relying upon the natural joy, dreamlike pleasure, and extra-ordinary realities opened up by creative play, we come to perceive that intuitive solutions and new possibilities for becoming constantly appear. Moving us into a larger context where the precise consciousness that normally orients us in waking reality is replaced by an expansion of physical or mental abilities, living *amor fati* allows us to begin to sense the larger shape of events and the timeless nature of our own existence. Providing learning experiences not otherwise available, where behavior and events can be judged against more developed and higher forms of understanding than those present in conventional daily reality at any level, *amor fati* directs the noble soul to discover the pure delight that Zarathustra's teachings associate with the innocence of the child and the levity of the Overman.

From a psychological perspective, understanding the ornithological freedom flight that inaugurates the living of *amor fati* allows us to clearly see one of the most insidious effects of Gravity: that what we take to be our own identity—our ego—has taken hold of and ensnared our becoming, preventing its diversification and maturation. Confronting the ego's tendency to universalize its own interests and needs as being good and right for others, the creative force of necessity at the heart of *amor fati* propels the noble soul to counter the arrogant and stubborn pride of the ego. Undermining the ego's tendency toward obsessions with forms of empowerment whose only purposes are perverse self-referencing and the debasement of others, *amor fati* encourages us to develop the capacity for moral freedom that can will deeds of love. Realizing itself in enactments of becoming that project us into the essentially generative quality of the world, *amor fati* contributes to a practical ethics that emphasizes mutual responsibility, social justice, and unconditional hospitality.

Finally, as a soul-spiritual path of individuation constructed around recognition of the transcendent function of the Self, the living of *amor fati* necessarily means opposing the realities of evil. Requiring creative resistance to the violent antipathies that precipitate bloodthirsty revenge and covert forms of terror, as well as to pathetic acts of acquiescence and profound boredom, the living of *amor fati* demands that we infuse life with unwavering compassion and an openness to radical contingency. It is through embodying these traits that the living of *amor fati* restores the innocence and relational interdependence that are the essence of cosmic-human love.

Amor fati, "love of fate," is intimately involved with the fate of love. As the cosmic force out of which being comes, love seeks expression and creativity. To love another, one must love oneself. As a living relationship that contains erotic, sexual, and heart-centered components, love is inseparable from devotion, loyalty, and trust. More concretely, to love someone, we must appreciate how that person differs from us and from others. We must learn to hold that person in mind so that to some extent love is a kind of meditation—a loving focus and creative exploration of the characteristics of the beloved, where even traits that would otherwise appear as faults are accepted and redeemed. As a form of intensely focused attention, love quickens the physical senses and alters our sense of time by deepening the joy of the moment even while seeming to emphasize the briefness of mortality.

Venturing to live the path of *amor fati*, we freely risk the fortune of our potentiality and surrender our fate to the always inexplicable vicissitudes of love. Because it emanates from the heart whose beat is the music of an organ of spiritual perception, opening to the vulnerability that comes with the experience of love, including the possibility of its loss, intimates an increased proximity to the Infinite. Since love brings us closest to a direct cognition of the nature of the Divine, when we affirm the living of *amor fati* we are affirming that the mysteries of love serve as the necessary ground of freedom through which we quest for our *unknown destiny*.

Conclusion

Coming to the end of our commentary on the textual song "Of the Spirit of Gravity," we see that "love of one's self" demolishes Zarathustra's enmity and the feeling of inferiority that binds him to self-pity and malevolence. Taking responsibility for his disgust at diseased humanity, Zarathustra facilitates our redemption from the ubiquity of violent revenge by calling forth the "unknown sage, the Self who rules and is ruler of the ego" (Z 62). His appeal to this eternal but invisible Self reflects his conviction that a "love of oneself" is necessary in order for the ego to release itself from the "unconscious envy" that regards life as "grown too late" for the overcoming of fate. Teaching that the heavy inheritance of fate can be dispersed by flights of freedom toward the possibility for pure awareness, Zarathustra reveals that the initiation of the Self is inseparable from the courage and innocence that allow one to live life as a destinal love song. With this disclosure of an essential connection between a "love of oneself" and the freedom for destiny living, we cross the bridge to becoming the Overman.

When Nietzsche assumes the lineage that protests the proliferation of Gravity in its modern nihilistic forms, he is aware that living *amor fati*, although available to everyone, is acceptable to hardly anyone. Undaunted by the apparently untimely aspects of living *amor fati* during our increasingly rancorous epoch, where we are exposed to and overwhelmed by self-consciously extreme and decadent lifestyles, Nietzsche commits to this psycho-philosophical path for the ennoblement of the soul, calling for the imbuing of the physical body and the earth with spiritual forces.

Perhaps prescient that the use of prosthetic-like teletechnologies for speeding up the "real time" of communication will become normalized, Nietzsche encapsulates the teaching of *amor fati* into a contemporary meditative practice:

1). Say *No* as little as possible. To separate oneself, to depart from that to which No would be required again and again.
2). *React as seldom as possible* and withdraw from situations and relationships in which one would be condemned as it were to suspend one's "freedom," one's initiative, and become a mere reagent. (EH 33)

Holding our imagination open to Nietzsche's meditative practices, whose affirmation arises from the negation of the negative, let us turn to and focus upon the declaration that Zarathustra offers as a culmination of his teaching. Facing scornful questions from both doubters and followers, Zarathustra remarks that it has been his fate to attain wisdom and to acquire a powerful taste for freedom by infusing the blood of life with unrestrained *truthfulness*. This fate has sent him on many journeys in consciousness, through many meditative traditions. Nonetheless, he specifies that his "ornithological" invocations to become light-full and weightless preach no doctrine other than the self-overcoming of Gravity. Moreover, he is adamant that he teaches only the alchymystical arts that contribute to a "love of one's self." Confronted by inquisitors whose self-absorbed need to know "The Way" is saturated with suspicion and cynicism and whose vulgarity of soul demands easy answers, Zarathustra remains defiant and singular until the final lines of his song. Refusing to insinuate himself as a new center of gravity for those pursuing a path of transformation, Zarathustra reiterates that his defiance of Gravity has required suffering and the undertaking of difficult flights of freedom along the paths of wisdom and love. Always teaching by a way of thinking that provokes new questions and requires deepening responsiveness, as well as further responsibility, Zarathustra declares, "This—is now *my* way: where is yours?"

But why, asks the crowd, must we find our *own* "way" of overcoming and transforming our egoism, our *own* "way" of cultivating nobility of soul? Zarathustra is unequivocal in his reply. Ever working to spur further initiations of our consciousness, he delivers a measured yet impassioned response, spoken with the deepest reverence for the cosmic mysteries:

"For *the* way—does not exist."

Postscript

> You say you believe in Zarathustra? But of what importance is Zarathustra? You are my believers: but of what importance are all believers?

> You had not yet sought yourselves when you found me. Thus do all believers; therefore all belief is of so little value.

> Now I bid you lose me and find yourselves; and only when you have denied me will I return to you....

> —Friedrich Nietzsche

Chapter 2

Zarathustra's Convalescence:
Cognitive Expansions and Inner Wisdom

WHILE OUR PREVIOUS study featured teachings for overcoming the dark and heavy instinct for revenge implanted in the
human soul by the Spirit of Gravity, it is only when we deeply listen to and
encounter Zarathustra's teaching "The Convalescent" (232–38), the song
of his most spiritual transformation, that we realize how the affirmation
of living *amor fati* entails traumatic wounding. This consideration is con-
firmed in our first meeting with Zarathustra: "One morning, not long after
his return to the cave, Zarathustra sprang up from his bed like a madman,
cried with a terrible voice, and behaved as if someone else were lying on
the bed and would not rise from it."

On the surface, which is not to be superficial, it seems safe to say that
even the "advocate of life, the advocate of suffering, the advocate of the
circle" is not immune to bad dreams. However, Zarathustra's wild and
uncontrolled wailing suggests a disturbance below the surface. Resisting
psychoanalytic interpretations that would classify his nocturnal affect
and imagery as pathological, we will regard his outburst as the undigested
aftereffects of his initiatic combat with the Spirit of Gravity. As evidence
that his initiatic encounter with this demonic force remains incomplete,
we will observe in this upsurge of night terror both the presence of his
alter ego, or Double, and the awakening of another possibility for being.

Beyond their value in helping us to understand *Thus Spoke Zarathustra*,
the teachings offered in "The Convalescent" are of the utmost importance

for contemporary human beings in our confrontation with the universalization of terror. Specifically, by turning our attention to the cause and dynamics of Zarathustra's self-diagnosed malady, "his great disgust at man," we will see how his experience of convalescence contributes to the development of a soul therapy that enhances individual health and the health of our relationships. By focusing on the practices that compose Zarathustra's convalescence, and by observing how elements of these practices are retained in works by contemporary philosophers, psychologists, and shamans, I will suggest that healing cannot be other than the immersion into the essential and eternal mysteries of love. In addition, by reading Zarathustra's teaching of convalescence as a path of return from the homelessness that has become the spiritual-earthly fate of all human beings, we will encounter fundamental aspects of soul wisdom necessary for the evolution of a modern form of initiation.

Recovering from his blood-curdling uproar, Zarathustra exclaims that the voice that spoke while he was outside himself came from his "abyss." Bravely, for our edification, he beckons his "most abysmal thought" near, though it disgusts him so deeply that, succumbing to nausea, he collapses into a deathlike stupor. "But when he again came to himself he was pale and trembling and remained lying down and for a long time would neither eat nor drink. This condition lasted seven days."

It is easy to discern in Zarathustra's paralysis of soul the great toll exacted by his unprepared encounter with his double. Awakening from his deathlike experience, Zarathustra is not only sickly, but also self-depriving in a way that points toward self-annihilation. Solitary, without close human relationships or friends, unable to experience strong positive feelings, and alienated from his physical body, he could easily be diagnosed with a "paranoid-schizoid personality disorder." While this diagnosis might be correct, I contend that Zarathustra's total non-communication and lack of participation in the external world are more appropriately understood as his willingness to undergo spiritual practices of detachment and purification. Oriented to the attainment of spiritually imagined self-knowledge, Zarathustra is aware that his convalescence, in addition to returning him to good health, must also enable him to fulfill his task as a transformation teacher. Consequently, this convalescence not only promotes the evolution of his healing but also inspires our contemporary knowledge-quest.

Animals, Kundalini: Fruit-plants, Shamanism

During this time of collapse and return Zarathustra is attended to by only "his" animals, the eagle and the snake. Accompanying Zarathustra since the beginning of his initiation, and loyal to him since his earliest awakenings and through his darkest hours, the eagle and the snake somehow belong to him. From this possessive categorization, a claim that has been duly observed by Heidegger, we may discern the animals' practical and symbolic significance.

According to Heidegger, Zarathustra's animals "want to know he is becoming the one he is, whether in his Becoming he finds his Being" (1984, 49). In his ontological project, Heidegger overlooks the subjectivity of Zarathustras's avowal that the *"proudest and wisest animals under the sun are scouting"* for him. In his concern to demonstrate a "closure to the history of metaphysics," Heidegger limits the complex relationship between Zarathustra and his animals to *their* need for security. His phenomenological method, directed at "constituting the basic stance of the teacher...and his mode of knowledge" (Ibid., 50), fails to capture the essence of the relationship that exists between Zarathustra and his animals. Limiting the "sensuous imagery" of this poetically forceful text to his concern with the "question of being," Heidegger misses the *curative* dimension of this relationship.

As a contrast to Heidegger's ontological approach, let us explore how Zarathustra's announcement of the presence of his animals, given in the prologue immediately before his initial downgoing, foreshadows the problematic of convalescence and transformation:

> *An eagle was sweeping through the air in wide circles, and from it was hanging a serpent, not like a prey but like a friend: for it was coiled around the eagle's neck.... I found it more dangerous among men then among animals; Zarathustra is following dangerous paths. May my animals lead me.*

From this description it is clear that the essential relationship between Zarathustra and his animals is intensely personal. To illuminate the complex symbolism in this relationship, we will turn to the seminar given by C. G. Jung in 1934–1939 on Nietzsche's *Zarathustra* (1988). Here is Jung's extremely helpful psycho-mythical commentary on the symbolic and enigmatic coupling between these two animals.

> Now he discovers his two animals, which were formerly explained as symbols of instincts. Usually the eagle, as an animal living in the air, has the quality of spirit, because spirit is understood to be a winged being, like an angel, a floating volatile being, or like the subtle body of a ghost, a *revenant*. Birds live on top of the highest mountains where nobody can go, or travel through the air, and that is always characteristic of spirit; to become spiritual one must rise out of the depths of heaviness, fast, and lose weight. And the snake is the symbol for the heaviness of the earth. It has no legs; it cannot jump or fly, but can only creep on its belly in the dust of the earth. And snakes often live in holes and in rocks, and some are nocturnal animals, uncanny. They lead a hidden existence and are met with where you expect them least. So the snake would be the symbol of the earth, for things chthonic. (Vol. 1, 227)

Let us amplify Jung's commentary by applying it to the therapeutic challenge that is at the heart of Zarathustra's convalescence. We have discerned in our previous study, "Of the Spirit of Gravity," that Zarathustra's self-initiation has included the "ornithological" experience of the Bird-Flight Meditation. Symbolized by the ascent of the eagle, the Bird-Flight Meditation is part of the path of soul strengthening that enables Zarathustra to undertake the mission of overcoming Gravity. If we are to understand the purpose of this mission and the role it plays in human evolution, we should neither interpret Zarathustra's involvement with the eagle to symbolize an attitude of inflated pride nor regard his doctrine of the Overman as advocating a delusional escape from earthly responsibilities. Rather, given Zarathustra's recognition of the passing of God and the inception of nihilism, his practice of the Bird-Flight Meditation reflects an awareness that only a therapeutic endeavor in which one learns how to loosen the subtle body's life forces from its enveloping material sheath can alleviate the downward pull of Gravity that so threatens the maturation of soul.

At this later stage of his convalescent journey, however, Zarathustra's inner development progresses by the unfolding of the Serpent Power Meditations. While again these teachings are not explicated in the text, it is our sense that Zarathustra has received their direct transmission from Lord Chance during one of his earlier wanderings, "Before Sunrise" (Z 186). When Zarathustra meets Lord Chance, the most venerable spiritual teacher of the ancient Indian wisdom, he has just experienced a night of "involuntary bliss," which has included "happiness and a woman"—yet in regard to the Heavenly Mysteries he remains innocent. Asking Lord Chance to clarify which actions he must undertake in order to teach humankind's overcoming of hostility toward the earth, and more subconsciously toward itself, Zarathustra receives the Serpent Power Meditations to awaken his thinking and strengthen his resolve. Aware that self-emptying is necessary for transformation, Zarathustra consciously enacts the practices of these teachings that call for coiling into inner and outer stillness. In undertaking these meditations, he chooses total renunciation.

To provide a fuller context for Zarathustra's healing through partaking of the Serpentine Arts, as well as for the reappearance of this ancient soul-spiritual tradition in contemporary healing efforts, let us sketch this aspect of the Wisdom of Ancient India. As taught to Zarathustra by Lord Chance, and as revealed in earlier writings such as the *Vedas* and the *Bhagavad Gita*, human beings of the Ancient Indian Epoch maintained continuity of consciousness with the presence of a Solar Being who was revered as the Cosmic Creator. Still capable of atavistic faculties of vision that connected them to the reality of a home more original than the earth, human beings of this epoch commonly regarded the world perceived by the physical senses as largely an illusion, as *maya*.

To guard against the risk of mistaking this materialist illusion for reality, Ancient Indian Wisdom meditates upon the Serpent, the animal that evokes the eternal mysteries of birth and death. Through its undulating movements and the shedding of its skin, the Serpent not only symbolizes the processes of growth and decay, it also reflects a structure capable of both receiving and emitting life forces. Correlating the ascending and descending movements of the Serpent to the structure of the human anatomy, Ancient Indian Wisdom found that the life forces flow along the vertebral column. While the subtle substance of this life force, which is called *kundalini*, is invisible to the physical eye, its path is mapped out according to a series of subtle sense organs, called *chakras*. Shaped as wheels or lotus flowers, these immaterial centers of consciousness and energy await purification and transformation by the meditative awakening of kundalini. Whether the method is yoga, visualization (*yantra*), chanting of vowels (*mantra*), gestures (*mudra*), sexual ecstasy (*tantra*), or the ingestion of sacred herbs and plants, the awakening of the kundalini signals an activation of health and wisdom.

In the Serpent Power Meditations taught to Zarathustra by Lord Chance, the kundalini, while asleep in the "root" chakra behind the genital organs and the anus, pulsates gently and continually. Meditation is focused on the breathing, so that through an intentionally regulated practice of expiration and inspiration the highly charged, chaotic air element, or *prana*, which maintains the whole body, is redirected downward. This descensional flow of *prana* has the effect of producing a gentle yet tangible warmth throughout and around the practitioner's physical body. When the meditatively enhanced warmth of the *prana* arrives at the delicate root chakra, the serpentine kundalini is aroused and begins to uncoil.

Ascending in wavelike flows and patterns from chakra to chakra, the serpentine kundalini at one and the same time absorbs and dissolves the subtle energies trapped in the matter of each center and emits its own potent potions. The self-potentiating dance of the serpentine kundalini becomes a dynamic force for stimulating an exaltation of the chakras, which in turn expands human self-awareness. And, as practitioner and practice become more concentrated, one comes to experience a melting of the identification with the limitations of the physical body, especially the obsession with sexuality. Facilitating an expansion of human self-awareness that makes perceptible the previously invisible body of formative forces, the undulations of the serpentine kundalini culminate in an enlightenment experience: human beings immediately apprehend that the surrounding ethereal environment is composed of a radiant light-force that serves to shelter the transferences of life vibrating between the human earth and spiritual cosmos.

We cannot underestimate the significance of Zarathustra's choice to convalesce by undertaking the Serpent Meditations. For when nothing less than his own physical-spiritual destiny is at stake, Zarathustra's choice to heal by awakening the kundalini is more than an acknowledgement of his loyalty to the "root" wisdom imparted in the exemplary teachings of Lord Chance, which he summarizes under the term "freedom from purpose." Rather, Zarathustra's path reflects his awareness that overcoming "his most abysmal thoughts," which are permeated by the qualities of disgust, pride, and condescension, necessitates physio-psychological changes that correspond to the powers of transformation symbolized by the Serpent.

The Serpent Power Meditations are not only important for Zarathustra's convalescence. Because he is an archetypal figure that personifies the evolutionary process of individuation, his choice offers symbolic indicators that resonate with the therapeutic challenges facing contemporary humanity in its epochal confrontation with all forms of terror. Because the serpent slithers unseen, suggesting cunning and betrayal, and because its most powerful self-protective mechanism is poison, suggesting venomous envy and pernicious evil, Zarathustra's involvement with these meditations discloses a path toward the integration of the shadowy parts of our personality. By practicing the Serpent Power meditations as a response to the undeniable exigency to transform the private madness that disturbs his sleep, torments his soul, and impedes his teaching mission, Zarathustra hazards that his "curse" can become a blessing.

Returning to the specifics of Zarathustra's convalescence, we have postulated that during his participation in the Serpent Meditations he has engaged in a seven-day fast. Following this purification process, we now observe a transitional activity that both previews his return to teaching and establishes the terms of relatedness between Zarathustra and his animals: he accepts the nurturing fruits they have procured. Although this gesture is overlooked by even as astute a reader as Lampert (1986), it is hardly an insignificant exchange. Heidegger notes that the "fruit-plants" offered to Zarathustra by his animals are symbolic, particularly in the colors of the "yellow and red berries." While Heidegger's association of yellow with "deepest falsehood" and red with the "supreme passion, of incandesecent creation" (1984, 51), is correct, he is preoccupied with identifying Zarathustra as the teacher of Eternal Return and with relating the colors of Zarathustra's fruits to the "question of Being." Our approach to these symbols, on the other hand, takes a foray into the biochemistry of the colorful berries and plants. As our concern is with Zarathustra's convalescence, we will ask if there is anything in the biochemistry of these "fruit-plants" that when ingested not only nourishes the hunger needs of the physical body but also stimulates the human neurosensory apparatus. Moreover, are there any properties of these "fruit-plants" that stimulate a breaking of our ordinary space-time continuum and animate uncommonly expansive and lucid psychic activity?

It is safe to assume that, with his gesture of smelling and taking the "rosy red apple" into his hands, Zarathustra has concluded his fast. It is our hypothesis, however, that this "fruit-plant" is hardly a safe food choice. Rather, we imagine this apple, which carries unmistakable Biblical overtones, to be the "food of the gods," a powerful psychoactive plant composed of a "fleshy, red skin cap sitting atop a yellow-white stem" (McKenna 1992). While we cannot know if Zarathustra is aware that ingesting this apple will stimulate his cerebrospinal fluids to promote transformations of consciousness and molecular reconfigurations, he clearly knows that his convalescence involves allies from other kingdoms whose purpose is to transmit benevolent spiritual influences. To substantiate our intuition that his choice to eat the apple furthers his healing, and to show how this choice reappears in contemporary therapeutic frameworks determined to promote an integral and process-oriented convalescence, we will refer to the work of R. Gordon Wasson and his associates.

A banker by profession and a mycologist by vocation, Wasson's primary importance for our study of Zarathustra's convalescence lies in his discovery of the presence and use of Soma, sacred mushrooms, in the initiation practices of ensouling consciousness in ancient India (1986). Developing this discovery through a textual analysis of the Sanskrit hymns known as the *Rig Veda*, undertaken with the help of mythologist and religious historian Wendy Doniger O'Flaherty, Wasson finds that *Soma* was a recurring presence during ritual meals. From this discovery, and from his researches into the Dionysian rituals at Eleusis, which yielded similar results, Wasson contends that "plant substances were and are at the very core of the Mysteries" (1978, 30). Additionally, his own experience of "fruit-plants" in their indigenous cultures, especially in Siberia and Mexico, allows him to advance a "unified field theory" of culture whose origin is neither human nor spiritual.

Beyond his innovations in ethnobotanical research, which link the pharmacological effects of these sacred plants together with their "religious" contexts, Wasson's work has two immediate consequences for a contemporary therapeutics of convalescence. First, Wasson is keen to distinguish the use of sacred botanicals in Mystery Centers from any contemporary indulgence in drug use and/or abuse. Consequently, Wasson, in conjunction with the classicist C. Ruck and the ethnobotanist Jonathan Ott, has coined the neologism *entheogen*, "god generated within" (1997), to denote "fruit-plants" that facilitate the attainment by human beings of extraordinary audio and visual rapture with the cosmos. Secondly, by challenging the classic and conservative analysis propounded by M. Eliade (1964), which puts forth the position that the historical degeneration of its ecstatic techniques no longer allows shamanism to provide viable healings, Wasson resurrects this soul wisdom tradition for contemporary investigation and experience. Maintaining that the ecstatic state associated with the healing practices of shamans was always enhanced by the use of entheogens, Wasson contends that shamanism remains a viable, if limited, means of curing both physical illness and maladies of the soul.

A crucial aspect of Wasson's research is his emphasis on the idea, weakly described in passing by Eliade, that the ecstasy of shamanic trance is essentially a *musical language*. The essential musicality of shamanic consciousness is given great prominence in Wasson's report of ingesting mushrooms with the Mazatec *curandero* Maria Sabina (Estrada 1981). More than an offering of her "oral autobiography," Wasson's description of Sabina's work also presents us with the healing chants of this unassuming and remarkable woman, whose soundings of ecstasy are both invitations and invocations to the Spiritual Beings of Light. As a witness to how these Light Beings transmitted their energies to this humble healer of human misery, Wasson also experienced their eventual transformation into forces of regeneration. To augment the authenticity of these shamanic rituals, let us note the work of Henry Munn, a poet with intimate knowledge of Mazatec shamanism. Munn asserts that a creative *symbiosis* with the mushrooms rests upon gaining a kind of molecular proximity to the formative-generative vibrations emitted by these plants. The result of attaining this symbiotic relationship is a linguistic experience where words are less data of information than containers of transformative energy that facilitate a concentration and expansion of consciousness to the point of an awakening to the sacred.

> The Indians do not call the mushrooms of light mushrooms, they call them the holy ones. For the shamaness, the experience they produce is synonomous with language, with communication, on behalf of her people, with the supernatural forces of the universe; with plentitude and joyfulness; with perception, insight and knowledge. It is as if one were born again; therefore their patroness is the Goddess of Birth, the Goddess of Creation. (Harner 1973, 99)

Zarathustra's Homecoming

Zarathustra's convalescence undergoes a clear alteration of mood and intensification of activity the moment he expresses his pleasure with the "rosy red apple," or *Soma*. Let us follow the textual narrative of this metamorphosis.

Taking his pleasure with the "fruit-plant" as a sign that the time has come to begin a dialogue with Zarathustra, his animals openly welcome the convalescent and encourage him to enter the world of things and beings. Yet their questions concerning the content of his knowledge quest, while hardly inappropriate, seem less a curious inquiry than an attempt to distract Zarathustra from becoming absorbed by the sights and sounds of his internal state. Attempting to quiet their own anxiety, they insist on telling Zarathustra who he is and what he must teach; they even speak of his destiny.

For his part, Zarathustra will have none of this identity theft and quickly interrupts his animals, calling them "buffoons and barrel-organs" and damning their oration as a banal "hurdy-gurdy song." He immediately rejects their claims to his knowledge on the grounds of attainment by wrongdoing. Like the human beings he denounces, they have become "spectators of pain" who, rather than learn from their own experience, try to appropriate wisdom by watching another's struggles. Finally, he announces that his sickness has initiated his most profound spiritual transformation.

Perhaps as the result of feeling the consciousness-expanding effects of the entheogen, Zarathustra now pours out twenty-two complete verses of introspective poetry that unfold a labyrinth of wisdom. Revealing again that his sickness unto madness has been necessary for his redemption, Zarathustra discloses that his abysmal thought "crept into my throat and choked me." Declaring that he "bit its head off and spat it away," Zarathustra acknowledges that he became acquainted with the monstrous nature of this thought while attempting to live in accord with the highest in human nature. Confessing his own tendency toward the weakness of "accusation," Zarathustra also professes what is most profound in his own learning, "that the wickedness in man is necessary for the best in him."

Beyond this insight, with Zarathustra's chant comes his recognition that convalescence necessitates overcoming the impoverishment of soul evidenced by his double disgust: "The greatest all too small—that was my disgust at man! And eternal recurrence even for the smallest! That was my disgust at all existence!"

Zarathustra's elaboration of his disgust at *man* concludes with the awareness that our acceptance of a humanity that ignores its true potential compels us to take revenge against the beauty of Nature, both external and internal. As a result of this accommodation, which is a character defect and a failure to manifest nobility of soul, the world is diminished and the self is degraded. Attaining freedom from his disgust at *existence*, Zarathustra realizes that Life requires the return of even the smallest and most pitiful. Consequently, Life demands that humanity affirm it just as it is, without blaming or complaining, and without recourse to abstract ideas about how it "ought or should be."

The completion of Zarathustra's "remembering his sickness," a highly emotional account of the trajectory of his spiritual transformation, brings neither consolation nor resolution. Exclaiming "disgust" three times, Zarathustra "sighs and shudders." Yet, at just this moment, when Zarathustra seems poised to proclaim the deeper sources of his redemption, the animals again become disruptive and interrupt his speaking. More than bad manners or ingratitude, their anxiety seems to reflect a preconceived idea that Zarathustra's remembering will culminate in a relapse. After all his personal experiences, however, Zarathustra knows otherwise and puts a stop to the interruption, telling the animals that they are behaving and speaking inappropriately. Expressing estrangement from their recitation of his teachings by twice emphasizing that his convalescence has been of necessity "self-devised," Zarathustra exclaims, "I must sing again." For Zarathustra now knows beyond any uncertainty that only the convalescent can sing the songs that will bring him "comfort."

At this moment of pivotal transition, when Zarathustra's convalescence seems to turn from lost to found, the animals continue speaking. Without expressing any reverence or gratitude for the profound generosity of their teacher, they continue to speak as if he were invisible. Their obliviousness to his lingering trace of disgust as he recalls the abysmal thought sinks to the point where they brazenly announce that Zarathustra is the Teacher of Eternal Return. More ominous than this indiscretion toward his private experience, which he now realizes is to become the path for the convalescence of humanity, are the final words of their recitation, which they offer as authoritative: "Thus—ends Zarathustra's down-going." Loyal until now, they betray him with this premature pronouncement of victory, out of fear that he will go mad and leave them again. Yet, even following their failed efforts to appropriate his experience, they still "expected that Zarathustra would say something to them."

Zarathustra's indifference to their plea coincides with his descent from the entheogen-aided consciousness journey. Moreover, his imperturbable presence signifies that while his convalescence has required him to internalize the instinctive and totemic functions of his animals, his health demands that he now sacrifice their company. Observing that their expectations for renewed teachings by Zarathustra are not to be fulfilled, the animals "respect" that his deepened meditative practices have yielded the great serenity that radiates from and around him. Seeing him surrounded by an aura of streaming rainbow colors, the animals are instinctively aware that Zarathustra's convalescence has taken a decisive turn, and they discreetly withdraw. For as the text now tells us, during this most intensely intimate moment of his convalescence, Zarathustra's impeccable silence discloses that he is "conversing with his Soul."

Conclusion

We can imagine that the supreme pathos animating Zarathustra's conversation with his soul, given in the text "Of the Great Longing," is Zarathustra's unfulfilled yearning for a more intimate experience of the self-awareness that is attained only through the mystery of relationship with the beloved. Repetitively and passionately intoning the expression "Oh, my Soul" twenty-two times (corresponding to the twenty-two verses of his inspired poem), Zarathustra is seeking nothing less than a confirmation that he has achieved "homecoming." Having incurred the woundings entailed by teaching the overcoming of Gravity and advocating the Overman, Zarathustra unequivocally embraces his soul, an act that rests upon his intuitive knowledge of its embodied and inspired wisdom. This heart-opening gesture, which manifests a never-before-acknowledged longing to achieve unity with his soul—and possibly intimacy with other human beings—reveals that his convalescence, and all true healing, can only come about through dissolving negative beliefs and reactive behaviors and activating emotional and cognitive capacities that proclaim a joyous affirmation of life.

Zarathustra's participation in this discourse reveals that the illness that first manifested as a disturbing nightmare is truly a darkening of the soul. As to the cause of this darkening, we have seen that it relates to his disgust, both at humanity for rendering itself small and at existence for the eternal repetition of this insignificance. Its origin, however, can be found in his belief in his helplessness and unworthiness. His attitude toward life contaminated by feelings of fear and hate, Zarathustra has been rendered incapable of taking an empathic interest in the fate and sufferings of others. His convalescence and teachings—and their significance for us—are contingent upon his attaining affective cognition that the fundamental essence of the soul is love.

How does Zarathustra's health compare to what Nietzsche says about the *great health* and its relation to what endures of Persian wisdom? Repeating an aphorism from section two of "Thus Spoke Zarathustra" in *Ecce Homo*, Nietzsche summarizes the psycho-spiritual characteristics of the individuality of Zarathustra: new ideals; new goals; the expanse of the soul and the wide spectrum of experience (his journey); continual self-creation (his going under); desire to explore the undiscovered and to confront "a world so overrich in what is beautiful, strange, questionable, terrible and divine" (his aesthetic cosmology); discontent with "present-day" man (his nausea over man); playfulness out of overflowing power and abundance (his gift-giving virtue); and "the ideal of a human, super-human [*Übermenschlich*] well-being and benevolence" (the Overman, the new meaning of the world). Thus Nietzsche describes Zarathustra as the one who most intensely abandons himself to living in the chaos and the conflict between the old and new moralities, and is in the process of creating new values. The aphorism ends by offering signs of the inception of a new world epoch where individuality expresses itself through a "multiplicity of character types" (Tuncel 2006): "the destiny of the soul veers round, time moves forward, the *tragedy* begins...."

Zarathustra can only come home to this "great health" and fulfill his destiny once he has turned his desire for union, if only for a moment, toward a conversation with his soul, whose receptive and transformative forces evoke his gratitude, deep thankfulness, and a new appreciation for the aliveness of all Creation. Hence Zarathustra's convalescence personifies the wisdom that it is only intimate relatedness to the abundance of nature, to the unfathomable mystery of others, and to our own inner being, that is curative to the soul. As an initiatic teaching for our time, if not all time, Zarathustra's convalescence is an affirmation of the wisdom that our soul is both eternal and woven spiritually out of love.

Chapter 3

WITH NIETZSCHE ON THE ROAD
FROM REVENGE TO REDEMPTION

For *that Man may be freed from the bonds of revenge*:
that is the bridge to my highest hope and a rainbow after
protracted storms.

—Zarathustra, "Of the Tarantulas"

To our strongest drive, the tyrant in us, not only our
reason but also our conscience submits.
  That which is done out of love always takes place
beyond good and evil.

—Nietzsche, *Beyond Good and Evil*

WHILE IT SEEMS unlikely that Nietzsche was possessed of clairvoyant consciousness, it is undeniable that he philosophizes as a visionary. Writing ahead of himself to those readers who can "endure his seriousness and his passions," Nietzsche envisions the future as the coming of nihilism, the devaluation to meaninglessness of all values heretofore deemed meaningful. Convinced that nihilism will reign as decisive in all aspects of social relations, Nietzsche warns that everyday life will be pervaded by an ineradicable *uneasiness*. He not only describes the specific characteristics of nihilism, such as the eclipse of reason by techno-scientism, the unbridled use of military and political power to expedite the spread of capital, and the substitution of fashion for individual authenticity and style; he also prescribes a way to resist its insidious and decadent amorality. Yet the consciously non-futuristic image he chooses for the foundation of his anti-nihilistic teachings can only be interpreted as provocative: "*The noble soul has reverence for itself*" (BGE #287).

We can accept Nietzsche's prescience based on our experience of the postmodern world. But, in order to accept the "self-reverence of the noble soul" as the image that animates our quest to defeat nihilism, we must—calling upon the understanding of nobility that we explored in Chapter One—adopt a way of being in the world that is animated by *heart thinking*. Heart thinking, which exceeds means-ends rationality, and whose appeal to truth rests upon the inner sense of direct cognition, has become necessary for Nietzsche perceives that the human *redemptive imperative* has grown weak, if not decadent.

This redemptive imperative is an active overcoming of the world-picture or ideology that privileges materialism and egoism by the attainment of soul-spiritual knowledge of the forces of Nature, both external and internal. It develops the capacity for freedom through which evolve the forces of cosmic-human love and wisdom necessary to balance the cosmic-human forces of evil. Furthermore, if we acknowledge that Nietzsche's prophetic vision of a future where nihilism penetrates and dominates the aesthetic, economic, political, and religious aspects of life is in fact the "fundamental problem" of the modern epoch, then regenerating the redemptive imperative in a way that allows for the maturation of the noble soul requires that we accept his claim "that psychology shall again be recognized as the queen of the sciences" (BGE #23). For psychology to achieve this recognition in the post-Nietzschean era of nihilism, however, requires that it relinquish its aspirations to be either a neurobiological theory of the mind or a therapeutics that overcomes psychosexual dysfunction by promoting the primacy of the ego. For, regardless of their intellectual sophistication, neither cognitive science nor relational or intersubjective psychoanalysis sufficiently addresses the nihilistic violence that fatigues our bodies and haunts our souls. On the other hand, it is possible for psychology to attain its regal status if it can find its way to a heart-thinking that activates the redemptive imperative to initiate both a moral-spiritual path of inner development and an ethics that is committed to social justice and responsibility toward others. Characterized by reverence, expansive generosity, hospitality, and, above all, selflessness, heart-thinking not only brings an enlivening "grandeur" to the face-to-face encounters between human beings, it also promotes the surfacing of possibilities for the psychological birth of the noble soul, whose inherent task is nothing less than to contest the spread of nihilism.

From Nietzsche to Zarathustra

To clarify Nietzsche's understanding of the redemptive imperative, let us turn to *Thus Spoke Zarathustra*. Here is the pertinent passage (pp. 160-61), poetically intoned by Zarathustra,

> I walk among men as among fragments of the future: of that future which I scan.
>
> *And it is my art and aim, to compose into one being together what is fragment and riddle and dreadful chance.*
>
> *And how could I endure to be a man, if man were not only also poet and reader of riddles and the redeemer of chance!*
>
> *To redeem the past and to transform every "It was" into an "I wanted it thus!"—that alone do I call redemption!*
>
> *..."It was"; that is what the will's teeth-gnashing and most lonely melancholy is called. Powerless against that which has been done, the will is spectator of all things past.*
>
> *The will cannot will backwards; that it cannot break time and time's desire—that is the will's most lonely melancholy.*
>
> *...This, yes, this alone is revenge itself: the will's antipathy towards time and time's "It was."*
>
> *...All "It was" is a fragment, a riddle, a dreadful chance—until the creative will says to it: "But I willed it thus!"*
>
> *...But has it ever spoken thus? And when will this take place? Has the will yet become unharnessed from its own folly?*
>
> *Has the will become its own redeemer and bringer of joy? Has it unlearned the spirit of revenge and all the teeth-gnashing?*

Zarathustra teaches that the source of revenge is the inability of the will to will backwards and to break "time's desire," which is the compulsion that drags us away from the present moment and imprisons us in the past. His concern is not with acts and feelings of revenge, which are basically only reprisals for previous acts and feelings of violence. Neither is this teaching involved with the wish to take revenge against the inevitability of physical death. Rather, for Zarathustra revenge is a disposition that springs from a condition the creative will finds intolerable: the inability to undo the past.

According to Zarathustra, "time's desire" is an unbearable humiliation that attacks the primordial openness of the creative will, restricting its role to that of an impotent spectator in its experience of "biography and history." In their inability to locate or generate any momentum for breaking through "time's desire," human souls are rendered increasingly inadequate to support the conservation of their *enthusiasms* (in Nietzsche's language, their life-energy). Severed from contact with any active forces that could influence the overcoming of "time's desire," human souls become resentful and vindictive, and revenge emerges as the sole outlet for the creative will. Under the inexorable demands of "time's desire," human souls become isolated, overwhelmed, and susceptible to all forms of repetitive compulsions that reveal antisocial tendencies.

In our effort to facilitate psychological understanding and to counter nihilism with the path of heart-thinking, we can understand revenge as the result of the willful refusal to forget. For when one persists in recalling the past's innumerable violations and unwarranted intrusions, yet resists taking any responsibility for those experiences, revenge seems justified. And even when one does manage to forget through repression or dissociation, a latent wish to remember remains and feeds the perpetual desire for revenge. Moreover, since revenge instills a lonely melancholy in the creative will, the determination not to forget perpetuates the impulse of self-reference. With this awareness, a hidden factor in the brutality of revenge is revealed: the affliction of narcissism.

Regardless of what form self-absorption takes, the narcissist is always sensitive to recrimination and always harbors resentment. For the narcissist, memories never pass away, and the unalterability of "time's desire" becomes fertile ground for the memorialization of bitter experiences. The fixation upon the failures and injustices of past relationships, and the attachment to an exclusionary love, suggest that the willful refusal to forget reflects a manic defense of the narcissist's undeserved feeling of specialness. Furthermore, the encapsulating subjective reference point of narcissism not only prevents the attainment of an awareness that could see the events of one's life as the unfolding of a field of interactive processes, it also forecloses the ability to meet the future creatively and imaginatively; instead, the future is determined by the past.

Binding the soul to objects and events from which it derives both envious frustration and vicarious gratification, the false self-assertion of narcissism impedes the ability to suspend reference to the past and risk true presence in the moment. Only by forgetting what we would otherwise memorialize, can we meet a person or situation as if for the first time, and engage in a beginning that breaks through the domination of time's desire. This leap into the unknown allows us to start our lives anew at every moment. Instead, unable to escape the looping and self-enclosing mechanism of negativity, the narcissist falls prey to fatalism. As a consequence of its inability to embrace life as a dance of destiny and to engage in the living of *amor fati*, narcissism inhibits the creative remembering that could allow our lives entrance to the newness of every moment. More pointedly, since the hyper-inflation of narcissism precludes the creative will from practicing the nobility of forgiveness—the soul quality necessary to surmount the tendency toward revenge—it reveals itself to be in the service of the nihilist project.

As the antidote to the obsession with exacting revenge, forgiveness is possible only if the narcissistic personality, which is entirely structured by self-interest, can "voluntarily and without the least injury to himself interrupt the stream of memory that bears his individual ego" (Prokofieff 1991, 43). Interrupting the stream of memory, which is identical to *forgetting* understood as a conscious break in the continuity of self-awareness, allows the narcissistic personality to renounce the tendency to blame, which is always fueled by rancor and is the precursor of seeking revenge. As a freely chosen subtraction undertaken in the solitude of the soul's truth, forsaking the tendency to blame, whether directed toward others who have perpetrated violence against us, or toward the self that has failed to live in accord with its own conscience, "always has a *sacrificial character*" (Ibid., 74). This means that forgiveness must be more than a temporary and ultimately recoupable loss on the part of the narcissistic personality. Forgiveness is only true when it reflects a self-overcoming, when the self comes over from narcissistic gratification to freely assume the obligation to return, to the others who populate our life and the otherness that is the world, a commensurate goodness for the violence that has been done to us or that we have wrought.

Forgiveness enables the soul to recollect itself emptied of hatred. In overcoming the solipsism of narcissism, forgiveness enables us to take an interest in others and to serve the world with a fully concentrated compassion. Practicing forgiveness enables us to transform the ordinarily distinct gestures of giving and receiving into a unified experience of communion and mutual self-realization. As the self-overcoming of narcissistic violence through the undertaking of freely willed actions of communicative and participatory service, forgiveness builds a bridge to Zarathustra's redemptive teaching by countering the vengeful attitude toward "time's desire." Against the passive habit of regarding "time's desire" through the lens of a resentful and resigned "It was," forgiveness affirms Zarathustra's creative proclamation, "Thus I willed it." When forgiveness operates as the driving moral force behind conscious self-willing, both within the self and between souls, the dynamics of power, which are always composed of mistrust and fear, are replaced by an ethics of responsibility that revolves around the quality of "*tolerance*" (Ibid., 50–51).

We have mentioned that Zarathustra's *prophetic vision* foresees a godless time when all aspects of personal and social life will become exposed to increasingly complex and destructive enmeshments, and a degenerating tendency will emerge from individuals' failure to freely choose moral values; especially forgiveness and the radical acceptance that defines tolerance. Facing these conditions, and in anticipation of confronting the "*spirit of revenge*" unleashed from all its traditional restraints, Zarathustra's transvaluative teachings aim to cultivate noble souls, capable of conscious and responsible willing, who have been educated in the arts of moral-spiritual living. In the wonderfully suggestive prologue to the work that bears his name, Zarathustra, proclaiming the human being as a bridge, ever coming and going, presents the "art of becoming." This initiatic path, which contains the attributes of courage, vulnerability (which is not to be confused with weakness, but is rather meant as openness), strength (which is not to be equated with power or manipulation, but is rather a sign of beauty), and the feeling for knowledge based on truth, is a theoretical template for infusing the discipline of psychology with heart-thinking as well as a practical way for us to realize forms of nobility that can reawaken the redemptive imperative.

With the recognition that Zarathustra's "art of becoming" intends to instruct the soul how to overcome the regressive and violent pull of "time's desire"—by affirming "I willed it" and engaging in acts of genuine forgiveness as the way to heal narcissistic wounding—we have illuminated the relation between nobility and the imperative to redeem ourselves from the compulsion for revenge. With this new awareness, we can now embark upon an exploration of one of Nietzsche's most provocative themes: the relationship between nihilism and Christianity. Given Nietzsche's thoroughly vitriolic attitude toward Christianity, the intention of our research, which is grounded in a reading of his *The Antichrist* (1979), is to liberate his hidden affirmation of the heart-centered spirituality that permeates the individuality of Jesus. Paying close attention to his "psychology of the redeemer," I will venture a most unlikely possibility: that in leading us to approach the cosmic teacher of peace and salvation who died on the cross freed from the attitude of revenge, Nietzsche guides us toward a contemporary western spiritual practice that can be perceived and assimilated by the noble soul in order to transform the course of human and planetary evolution from terror to love.

From Zarathustra to *The Antichrist*: Nietzsche's Psychology of the Redeemer

We have indicated that Nietzsche's writings assume the task of regenerating the redemptive imperative. Moreover, according to his own self-understanding, Nietzsche writes to those singular readers of the future who will resist the nihilistic petrifications of life by insisting upon a fully human and individual freedom. Regardless of his intention to contribute to these dual actualizations, it is all too easy to misunderstand *The Antichrist*, which on the surface is entirely hostile to Western religious belief, as endorsing the nihilism that Nietzsche so deeply disdains. His proclamations of "contempt for the wretched of the earth" make it all too easy to characterize Nietzsche as an anti-religious thinker. Yet it is my sense that the teachings of *The Antichrist*, while obviously offering a critique of religion, are inseparable from Nietzsche's desire, however veiled, that modern souls contest the godlessness of nihilism by aspiring toward the development of a spiritual life. In fact, as early as the text's foreword, Nietzsche encrypts an eightfold path of moral behavior and psycho-spiritual affirmation. The following key terms, gleaned from the text, form this path:

1) Strength that prefers daring questions.
2) Courage for the *forbidden.*
3) Predestination for the labyrinth.
4) An experience out of seven solitudes.
5) New ears for new music.
6) New eyes for the most distant things.
7) A new conscience for truths that have hitherto remained dumb.
8) The will to economy in the grand style: to keeping one's energy, one's *enthusiasm* in bounds.

As we attempt to understand the implications of this path against the background of Zarathustra's teaching against revenge, offered in "On Redemption," let us note that Nietzsche locates his stimulus for writing *The Antichrist* in the "sighing resignation," the "virtuous uncleanliness," and the lack of courage toward soul-spiritual principles characteristic of modern souls. Nietzsche implores his future readers to understand that these symptoms of decline are inculcated by the propaganda machinery of the clerical army. Directing his strongest negative animus at the ecclesiastical power holders and ideologues of the Church, the social institution most responsible for the decadence of the redemptive imperative,

Nietzsche is especially critical of those religious doctrines that command extending a "bloodless" neighborly love to all other human beings. Not surprisingly for one whose moral path is "predestined for the labyrinth and the experience of seven solitudes," Nietzsche can only view the Church, which "calls itself the religion of pity," as a monolithic institution that substitutes obedience to dogma for conscious self-willing, thereby inhibiting the attainment of *reverent nobility*.

Once he has expressed the force of his enmity against the Church and its theological sublimation of human passions, Nietzsche's attention comes to "touch on the problem of the *psychology of the redeemer*" (AC #28):

> ...What *I* am concerned with is the psychological type of the redeemer....*Not* the truth about what he did, what he said, how he really died, [or in how] it has been "handed down" by tradition, but the question *whether* his type is still conceivable at all. (AC #29)

After a cursory examination and dismissal (as having little relevance to psychological type) of the two "*physiological realities*" upon which the Church's doctrine of redemption has grown, "*instinctive hatred of reality*" and "*instinctive exclusion of all aversion, all enmity, all feeling for limitation and distancing,*" Nietzsche is convinced he has "anticipated that the type of the redeemer has been preserved for us in only a very distorted form" (AC #30–31). Citing the lack of a cultural milieu for comprehending the appearance and experience of an Enlightened Being in human physical form, and the tendency for exaggeration by both true believers and skeptics, Nietzsche asserts that the traditional Church descriptions perpetrate a mass delusion. He points to the way Church "semiotics and metaphor" reduce the living ardor of blessedness and the arrival of "glad tidings" to a state of being where "there are no more opposites" and a structure of faith that reflects a kind of "childishness in the spiritual domain" (AC #32). Finally, he presents Jesus as a kind of savant, born enlightened, whose teachings are not "won by struggle." Consequently, Church doctrine, with its emphasis on effort and renunciation, is unable to fully receive and transmit the glorious illumination and unfettered becoming of the redeemer; instead, its religiosity *betrays* the intentions of this being "whose every moment is its own miracle, who *lives*, resisting formulas...not tied to any conditions" (Ibid.).

After his thorough deconstruction of the illusions perpetrated by the Church about Jesus, it would hardly be surprising if Nietzsche failed to keep his discoveries in "good bounds." Yet, rather than celebrate his position, Nietzsche submits his findings to the aesthetic, psychological, and religious principles of his own moral-spiritual path. Demonstrating his "strength for daring questions," Nietzsche—contrary to his critical views toward the Church, and most definitely against his own instinctual and intellectual inclinations—begins to entertain the possibility that certain of Jesus' qualities of soul can incarnate in contemporary human beings. As to the source of this new feeling, it seems that Nietzsche has come to see Jesus not simply as exemplifying an attitude of life-denying renunciation, but also as having lived a life wherein "there lies concealed one of the most painful cases of the martyrdom of *knowledge about love*" (BGE #269).

Perhaps in possession of "new eyes for the most distant things," Nietzsche goes so far as to call Jesus a "free spirit," and describes the redeemer as an "unprecedented affirmation," whose presence radiates such goodness and healing power that even those who cannot understand his words must feel it. Indeed, Nietzsche describes Jesus as "a being immersed in symbols and incomprehensibilities" (AC #32)—symbols, such as the "Kingdom of God," that are precisely an expression of the freedom of spirit, the transformative capacity that Nietzsche finds so wonderful in human beings. What is significant about Jesus for Nietzsche is not the metaphysical reality of Father, Son, and Kingdom of Heaven, but the redeemer's luminous "condition of the heart" (AC #34). This condition makes blessedness possible here and now by the practice of a divine life that is "incapable of *denial*, lacks the need for dialectical proof, and speaks only of the most inmost thing: 'life' or 'truth' or 'light'" (AC #32).

We have seen that Nietzsche has called the ignorance of the less enlightened a temptation to revenge, hence it is in a mood of profound empathy, and perhaps identification, that he wonders how the being of the redeemer absorbed the psychological immaturity of his disciples and followers. He also ponders whether his flock has been able to grasp the transfigurative knowledge-feeling experiences offered by the redeemer's teachings and example. While Nietzsche concludes that the historically unfavorable material and spiritual conditions made distorted understandings inevitable and therefore forgivable, he insists that his companions' ignorance "must in any case have *coarsened*" Jesus—aging his spirit, in a sense, much as the body ages, becoming brittle and less fluid. Nietzsche then goes on to assert that for the unique being who was Jesus, "the *consequence* of such a condition projects itself into a new *practice*, the true evangelic practice."

Despite the offence of *coarsening* to the redeemer's spirit through passive incomprehension or overt attacks, this *practice* turns away from revenge. Jesus is subjected to and affected by relentless scorn and repetitive violence, yet He intervenes in the affairs of human beings to divert oppositional forces from conflict in the outer world and to harmonize the soul's own divided and divisive inner impulses. In fact, it is this very *coarsening*, Nietzsche suggests—which subjects Jesus to the battle of settling inwardly the antagonisms between Fear and Love that would otherwise flow through thinking, feeling, and willing into the external world—that makes possible the sublime equanimity that streams forth from the redeemer.

The *consequences* of the redeemer's experience of *coarsening* are most visible in the miracles of healing. For it is through Jesus' consciousness of the transgressions that caused the hardening of the spirit within his own body that his non-intrusive touch of revitalization affirms the faith it proclaims. Moreover, these healings, which are the most demonstrative *consequence* of his teaching, reveal to the healer and the healed that it is through the *practice* of one's life that one feels "divine," "blessed," "evangelic," at all times a "child of God." "It is *not* 'penance,' *not* 'prayer for forgiveness' which leads to God; *evangelic practice alone* leads to God, it is God" (AC #33). As an evangel and free spirit, Jesus practices a life of blessedness that is without sin and without *ressentiment*; neither yearning to return to an earlier state of spiritual consciousness nor seeking the promise of an unperturbed afterworld. Rather, Jesus teaches the Eternal as the birth of an unprecedented way of conjoining with the Divine in this life. From the healings that give rise to the sense of immortality as well as the teachings that sanctify eternal life, it becomes clear why Nietzsche concludes, in a way that bears directly on how *coarsening* activates the creative will, that the "psychological reality of the redeemer" is specifically "a new way of living, *not* a new belief" (Ibid.).

Given his awareness of the *coarsening* that accompanies the redeemer's physical and spiritual ministry, it is not surprising that Nietzsche maintains that the teachings of this "new way of living" are given in accord with a *practice*. We can only speculate as to whether Jesus' *practice*, as read by Nietzsche, has influenced the path of inner development encrypted in the foreword to *The Antichrist*. However, there is no doubt that his desire for the cultivation of soul qualities capable of embodying a contemporary manifestation of the redeemer type finds support in our decryption of his less than explicit practice. Toward the inception of a "new way of life" that counters the "universalization of terror," let us discern, with Nietzsche, the distinguishing characteristics of the only Christian *practice*, the one Jesus "bequeaths to mankind, as he died, as he lived, as he *taught*"—

> *Not* to defend oneself
> *Not* to grow angry
> *Not* to make responsible...
> *Not* a belief but a doing,
> above all a *not*-doing of many things,
> a different *being* ...
> *Not* to resist even the evil man—
> But to *love* him... (AC #35–39)

As a response to the realities of nihilism, whose major symptoms include the vicissitudes of violence and revenge as they come to manifestation in materialism and egoism, Nietzsche's psychology of the redeemer reveals a living practice whose sacrifices culminate in the affirmation of *amor fati*. From our consideration of Nietzsche's thinking concerning the "psychological type of the redeemer," we can both imagine Jesus as the archetype of the *noble soul* and also see that psychology, by surrendering its commitment to bolstering ego-centeredness and by embracing the above practices as a way toward the path of heart-thinking, can become "now once again the road to the fundamental problems" (BG#23).

By incorporating the redeemer's *practice*, the therapeutic aspect of psychology can be reoriented from a discipline concerned with ameliorating the dysfunctional patterns derived from instinctual and object aims, and psychotherapy can become an initiatic path that liberates us from the desire for revenge. As the logic of our post-Nietzschean psyche becomes animated by and identified with the inner processes that compose soul life as it mediates between body and spirit, the maturation of "I"-consciousness—the essence of the self—emerges as a core component of the redemptive imperative that grounds all therapeutic endeavors. As to the realization of "I"-consciousness, which Nietzsche symbolizes as the "experience of seven solitudes predestined for the labyrinth," this evolution can be accomplished only if the therapeutic and/ or initiatic path succeeds in enveloping the egoistic tendency to self-centeredness within the circulating warmth of heart-thinking. Inspired by cosmic-earthly love, the expanded range of perception afforded by heart-thinking brings the multidimensional "I"-consciousness of the Self into contact with already present cosmic-earthly wisdom in order to embark upon a healing of the self-other-world matrix.

From Nietzsche's *Antichrist* to Steiner's Christ Impulse

Our reading of Nietzsche's *The Antichrist* has been concerned with showing the influence of the redeemer's *practice* on the psychological birth of noble souls, especially its contribution to an "I"-consciousness whose development includes the new capacity for heart-thinking. Additionally, confronted by Nietzsche's prophecy of a nihilism that will be fueled by instinctive violence and forms of self-absorbed aggrandizement and desolation, we have pursued his question of whether the type of being that came to incarnation in Jesus can attain a contemporary manifestation.

In doing so, however, we must acknowledge that Nietzsche's psychology of the redeemer, perceptive as it is, can only be understood as a failure. Enclosed within the intellectual milieu of his times, the materialism of which made it impossible for him to cognize the existence of supersensible worlds and beings, Nietzsche's psychology inevitably reduces Jesus to an exceptional "type" of a human being without ever coming to a true comprehension of the Christ.

Having yet to answer the question of whether a contemporary manifestation of the redeemer is possible, our investigation moves beyond Nietzsche's humanism toward Rudolf Steiner's abiding and multidimensional considerations of the Mystery of Golgotha. While the specific ways in which Steiner's work animates the creative exigency at the heart of modern initiation will be the focus of the second part of this book, a preliminary characterization of his researches into the Mystery of Golgotha is pertinent here, not only because they address the questions posed by Nietzsche's philosophical psychology, but also because they are concerned with how the world-picture of nihilism, which is a manifestation of the problem of evil, calls forth the reawakening of the human redemptive imperative. In our examination of Steiner's spiritual science, gaining a living relationship to the Mystery of Golgotha becomes indistinguishable from the rehabilitation of the redemptive imperative.

Within the multiple contexts of Steiner's researches, we will briefly refer to his lecture of May 2, 1913, "Christ at the Time of the Mystery of Golgotha and Christ in the Twentieth Century." In this lecture Steiner emphasizes the uniqueness of Christ's sacrificial deeds, pointing out "that a Being who in the realm of His own will could never have experienced death... descended to the earth in order to undergo an experience connected inherently with man" (1966, 27). Through Christ's union with the body of Jesus of Nazareth and His death on Golgotha, a Being who previously belonged to the cosmos entered into the very process of earth's evolution, and since then "He lives with the souls of men and with them experiences life on the earth" (Ibid., 28).

The Mystery of Golgotha reveals that the spiritual light of the cosmos, which ancient peoples always associated with the sun and which is one with the Christ, has entered into the history and atmosphere of the earth, *"imparting to the earth its meaning and purpose"* (Ibid.). In the recent path this revelation could be accepted or rejected on faith alone. But following the evolution of consciousness that has, paradoxically, given us increased individual freedom as well as the abstract and intellectualized form of thinking that dominates life in the age of nihilism and represses revelation, we must now take a different approach. A human relationship to the Mystery of Golgotha in our time must be guided by the *attainment* of spiritual knowledge—a comprehensive practice that reveals the interweaving of divine and earthly life. This contemplative activity demonstrates to us our independence from physical matter and enables us to recognize our unique individual multidimensional identity. At the core of this knowledge, and of fundamental importance for gaining a living relationship to the Mystery of Golgotha, is the awareness, beyond all messianic hopes and mystically-inspired claims of a second coming, that Christ will not reappear in a physical body (1983a, 84). (This contemplative activity is far indeed from the passive waiting for Christ's return that leaves us vulnerable to the delusions of false prophets.) Moreover, since gaining a living relationship to the Mystery of Golgotha is particularly challenged by the cynicism and skepticism that are endemic to nihilism, its attainment depends upon our conscious efforts to overcome any tendency that advocates joining a church or following church doctrine in the hopes of achieving salvation. Rather, it is only through our individual, freely acquired cognition of Christ's deed of incarnation and resurrection, of His entry into life and His vanquishing of death, that the renewal of the Mystery of Golgotha as an ongoing and incomplete event of spiritual-human creativity and transfiguration can lead us across the abyss of existential nothingness and materialistic emptiness.

To find the Christ in the epoch of nihilism is the task of noble souls. Yet if noble souls are to find the Christ, they must find Him in freedom. In our age of the "universalization of terror," noble souls can find the Christ only through freely undertaking the responsibility of cultivating their own human forces and developing inner senses, especially the capacity for heart-thinking. If this effort at spiritual maturation remains faithful to (re)cognizing how the light of the Christ shines forth from all that is living, we can overcome the deadening effects of an abstract science that is concerned exclusively with mastering the natural world. At the same time, we can resist an instrumental rationality that would limit the play of consciousness to the highly specialized functioning of an outwardly directed and power-motivated ego. Moreover, it is only by finding the Christ in acts of freedom that noble souls are able to transcend the forces of decline—typified by Nietzsche as those who uphold the morality of good and evil, such as the sage that teaches virtue, the priest and the despisers of the body—and enter into the forces of ascent, typified by Nietzsche as those who create values beyond good and evil, such as the wanderer, the warrior, the artist-dancer, and of course the Overman.

To undertake this ascensional path of freely finding the Christ is to selflessly serve the redemptive imperative. When noble souls choose to devote themselves to enacting light-filled and creative deeds of love, peace, and charity, they contribute to the task of overcoming the meaninglessness of nihilism and recovering for humanity its purpose in the universe. Enacting these gestures, which point toward the Infinite and the Eternal while coming to manifestation in the commotion and commerce of everyday life, the noble soul can attain to a certain resurrection of his or her own being, and, instead of longing for a contemporary incarnation of Christ, become *oneself* a being filled with Christ.

Chapter 4

TRAUMATIC PAIN:
PSYCHOTHERAPEUTIC CONVERSATION
BETWEEN MEDIUMSHIP AND SOUL WISDOM

We are now approaching a time when, in addition to the already evolved self, certain clairvoyant faculties will again evolve quite naturally. Human beings will have the strange and remarkable experience of not knowing what is really happening to them! They will begin to receive premonitions that will become reality, and they will be able to foresee events that will actually take place. Indeed, people everywhere will gradually begin to actually see, although only in shadowy outline and in its first elements, what we call the etheric body. The human being of today sees only the physical body; the capacity to see the etheric body will gradually be added. People will have learned that this etheric body is a reality, or they will think it is an illusion of their senses, since such a thing, so they will say, does not exist. Things will come to a point at which many people who have such experiences will ask themselves, "Am I really mad?"

—Rudolf Steiner, January 27, 1910

THE EVOLUTION in consciousness that Steiner envisions comes with an explicit challenge: either we enhance the natural development of clairvoyant faculties, especially the ability to behold the reality of the etheric body—the invisible body of life-forces which holds the form of the physical body together—or our newly experienced cognitions will be denied as illusory, or worse yet, drive us toward madness. How psychotherapists and other healers of the soul respond to this challenge depends not only upon whether we believe in the reality of non-ordinary experiences, such as premonitions becoming actual and other synchronous events, but, most importantly, on our understanding of and response to trauma.

Psychotherapists normally confront trauma in the form of residues of severe childhood abuse, or as the result of the unavoidable and unexpected losses and displacements that occur during adulthood. Always catastrophic, trauma spawns affect storms filled with rage, dread, annihilation anxiety, and grief. Traumatic wounding, which always deforms the subjectivity of the self, often leads to further fragmentation into layers of complex false-self organizations, and to a compromise of intersubjectivity where self-other connections are severed, hidden and cohere around antagonistic polarities. Contrasted with these psychic experiences, in which toxic insensitivity, sadistic domination, and forms of destruction whose cruelty may be impossible to assimilate contaminate the relational milieu, Steiner's vision of a transition in consciousness that encompasses spiritual realities and beings may appear harmless. Yet this mutation in consciousness, which signals the movement from an exclusive reliance upon sense perception to gain knowledge of the manifest world to the arising of creative imaginations that offer knowledge of the previously invisible or spiritual world, is no less disruptive than physical and emotional violence.

How, then, can the self accommodate the shocking newness of the knowledge experience announced by Steiner? Furthermore, how can the self welcome this transition in consciousness as a call toward creative transformation without resorting to defensive patterns of dissociation? As a preliminary answer to these questions, I would suggest that psychotherapists must open their theories to new understandings of the human being and their practices to new forms of relating and communicating. Toward this event of dual opening, psychotherapists must allow themselves to experience, during every session, a process of *surrender*.

The psychotherapeutic process is often a daunting practice of enduring the patient's need to dissemble and withhold. In this practice, where the presence of trauma marks the reality of unendurable suffering, the therapist's surrender of apparent well-being eases the patient's pain of giving a more truthful account of himself. Indifferent to theoretical orientation, the therapist's surrender disperses the discipline of technique in favor of the continuous exercise of *yielding to unknowing*. This surrender is not, however, a form of negation. In fact, it is a type of revolt, especially against one's own ideas, one's own resolutions and plans, and assuredly against the comfort of one's own intelligence, sensibilities, and sanity. As the omnipresent background mediation of therapeutic practice, surrender facilitates the attunement of mood necessary for encountering the relationship failures that characterize traumatic disorders. While surrender may precipitate temporary disorientation, the therapist's relinquishing of preconceptions optimally positions the psychotherapeutic conversation to search for the new points of orientation that give this healing endeavor its meaning.

The therapist's surrender of the position of the omniscient object allows the psychotherapeutic process to expand from an exclusive reliance upon restorative interpretations. Likewise, the therapist's surrender of the role of the all-powerful director allows the patient's unmetabolized trauma and self-defeating character patterns to be approached and related to through non-intrusive inquiry, empathic commentary, responsive recognition, and creative participation. From this communicative activity, which both embodies the modern project of self-narration and self-consciousness and encourages the wish to expose one's deepest secrets, there emerges an open space for shared experience and the mutual correcting of seemingly exclusive and antagonistic attitudes and beliefs. Victor Turner, an anthropologist who has studied ritual process and performance enactments, calls this open space

> ...an interfacial region, or to change the metaphor, an interval, however brief, of *margin* or *limen*, where the past is momentarily negated, suspended, or abrogated, and the future has not yet begun, an instant of pure potentiality, when everything, as it were, trembles in the balance. (1982, 44)

The reality of the "interfacial region" has been made known to psychotherapists by Winnicott's idea of a "transitional or potential space" (1971), as well as through Schwartz-Salant's imagination of the "subtle body" (2007). Awareness of the transitional space of the "interfacial region" in therapeutic work with traumatized patients, which regularly exhibits eerie vibrations, moods of high anxiety and apprehension, conditions of extended inconclusiveness, obsession with security, and temporary sense-perceptive dissonance, allows for imaginative insight and mutual understanding to emerge from whatever internal and interpersonal experiences are flowing "in between" both participants. As the site of "pure potentiality," the "interfacial region" promotes the therapeutic work of establishing a true dialogue where new meanings and identifications are created, destroyed, and recreated within the safety of a mutually transformative relationship.

Therapeutic Pathways: Bromberg, Steiner, Torok

In order to provide a larger context for the ways in which the "interfacial region" of psychotherapeutic conversation can attempt to mitigate the potentially traumatizing effects occasioned by the opening of the supersensible world, let us look at the work of Philip Bromberg. Having written extensively and empathically about the psychotherapeutic process with patients who have experienced trauma, Bromberg notes that their narratives are dominated by the defenses of "insularity, self-containment and an avoidance of spontaneity or surprise" (1998, 9). These severely disturbed patients not only resist participation in a dialogic conversation, but punctuate their communication with "gaps, black/blank holes, zoning out and disruptive instances of discontinuity in and between self-narratives and patterns of relating" (Ibid., 9). Alongside his allegiance to the contemporary psychoanalytic view of "the self as de-centered, and the mind as a configuration of shifting, non-linear states of consciousness," Bromberg describes these patients as constituting themselves through a "defensive division of the self into unlinked parts ... each with its own boundaries and its own firm experience of not-self" (Ibid., 12). For psychotherapy to gain inroads into the defenses of these patients, whose tormented pasts have deprived them of the illusion of unitary selfhood, the therapist needs to demonstrate respect for each of these "unlinked parts" without capitulating to the reality of any single part.

It is crucial for the therapist to remain non-judgmental toward this pathological structuring of the self if the psychotherapy is to avoid reactivating forms of indoctrination and enforced compliance. In addition to providing a safe and non-critical environment, the therapist also needs to recognize that the overall dissociative form of organization is an expression of the precariousness of existence. Working from within this recognition requires that the therapist surrender any recourse to abstraction and any feelings of absolute difference; thus, this process leads beyond the accumulation of information to the achievement of an intuitive "seeing into." The importance of this form of recognition, which is really a mode of perception, is that only through intuitive "seeing into" does it becomes possible for the therapist to grasp the underlying reason why psychotherapy with these patients takes place as if in each moment everything "trembles in the balance." For the truth of dissociation, regardless of its symptoms and strategies of dissimulation, is that it always carries the seeds of absence that intimates death.

Intuitively "seeing into" the work of death which is hidden in dissociative pathologies allows the psychotherapeutic conversation to move from serial and unintegrated interactions to a dynamic process of "interfacial" exchanges. In these dialogic searches for the patient's nonexistent self, where the mere act of exposure is fraught with terror, the therapist must be able to tolerate and acknowledge breakdowns in rapport. Bromberg describes this capacity as the "ability to stand in the spaces between realities without losing any of them—the capacity to feel like one self while being many" (Ibid., 186); and he emphasizes the necessity of this approach if patients are to risk allowing what has been both unknown and prohibited to enter the psychotherapeutic conversation. Playing attentively and relating within the "interfacial region" not only diffuses the threat of destruction posed to the protective shells of the patient's unconscious, it also ameliorates the anticipated destructiveness of therapeutic relatedness. The process of dynamic exchange permits the patient to recognize hateful, vengeful, and demonized aspects of the self without fear of reprisal. By coming closer to the marginalized feelings at the boundaries of the patient's exiled self without transgressing his or her privacy, working within the "interfacial region" invites the patient to use the psychotherapeutic conversation as an open space to explore the pain and shame that were unapproachable when survival was the best one could hope for.

Steiner

Taking as a background the role of the "interfacial region" in psycho-therapeutic conversation with patients suffering from trauma, we can begin to engage with Steiner's psychological researches, especially as they concern the advent of the new stage of consciousness that he calls "etheric clairvoyance" (1983a). Steiner constructs his psychology upon a phenomenology of the self that understands the human being to be composed of body, soul, and spirit. He understands the soul—as the aspect of the self that most immediately pertains to the discipline of psychology—to be an interior, involuted world that contains within itself all the qualities that reveal themselves in the universe. Steiner also proposes that the soul exists in a polar relationship with everything with which it is connected. Continuously in movement between the various poles, it is nevertheless inwardly consistent (invariable).

Beyond these essentialist descriptions, Steiner's psychology presents an inner path for transformation that rests upon a complex understanding of the relationship between the soul and the uniqueness of the modern epoch, (beginning approximately 1413–1429 C.E.). While hardly alone among cultural critics of the late nineteenth and early twentieth centuries, Steiner maintains that human beings of the modern epoch shape their economic, political, and social relations within philosophies of materialism. Parallel to this development, the modern epoch requires knowledge to become associated with acuity in intellectual analysis. As a consequence, the Cosmic "I", the spiritual force that had previously given humanity guidance, has become either veiled or forgotten (1997a). Moreover, because of the successes of the materialistic world-view and its natural scientific discoveries, the modern human being is compelled to confront the self-other-world totality by means of personal cognitive forces that depend solely on outer sense perceptions. Linking sense-based perception to the development of an increasingly abstract rationality has led humanity to the discovery of logical laws and the invention of techno-scientific means that increasingly dominate life on earth. Assimilating these discoveries and inventions into an economy motivated by the circulation and accumulation of capital, whose material achievements are indisputable, the intellectual consciousness of post-theological humanity has naturally come to prize most of all its freedom from external spiritual interference.

Steiner acknowledges that the maturation of the intellect and the enhancement of freedom during the early modern period necessitated the suppression of spiritual awareness and intuitive (clairvoyant) capacities. He concludes, however, that by the end of the nineteenth century, the mental-physical consolidation of the human being had come to completion. Moreover, by the beginning of the twentieth century, Steiner, like many social critics and artists, discerned that the exclusively earthbound gravitational pull of materialism had begun to generate counter-tendencies. Aesthetic movements as disparate as Cubism, modern dance, and atonal music, as well as Einstein's scientific discoveries and the militaristic-nationalistic impulses that eventually led to the First World War and the Bolshevik Revolution, arose to challenge the epistemological certainty that supported the modern worldview. Yet perhaps the most significant indication that intellectual consciousness based on sense perception had reached a point of critical instability was Freud's invention of psychoanalysis and the discovery of the unconscious.

Steiner was acutely aware of psychoanalysis and viewed its existence as an indication that the consolidating forces propelling materialism had peaked. Accepting the validity of the unconscious as a source of meaning and suffering, Steiner nevertheless viewed psychoanalysis as a symptom of a transition in consciousness. For him, the key to this transition lay in the "threshold" experience: an awakening of awareness that reveals the interconnection between the human life-world and the spiritual cosmos (1987). From this spiritual perspective, it is clear why Steiner objected to the popular reduction of the unconscious to an exclusive concern with subconscious instincts and impulses. More importantly, Steiner felt that the central presupposition of psychoanalysis, which is that sexuality is the causal principle in human functioning and relating, reduces human beings to their physical nature and neglects their spiritual aspect. He further objected to the fact that while its treatment of neuroses overtly relies upon language, its theory of illness perpetuates a biological materialism that denies healing power to the Word. Beyond these and other criticisms of psychoanalysis (1990), Steiner's researches have revealed that the characteristic functions of the soul are irreducible to the constitutional structure of the body and that the human being is more than its visible physical aspect. Rather, the human being, in addition to its physical body, also consists of invisible or supersensible sheaths, which Steiner calls the etheric, astral, and ego bodies (1997a).

Steiner's understanding of the bodily constitution, and of its relation to states of the soul, immediately reconfigures our understanding of the self and redefines the contours of the human encounter. Working from within this new topography, we can observe that our first impressions of sympathy and antipathy are gleaned from contact with the physical appearance of the other. Emotions, which are essentially preferences, are usually quick to appear, especially at times of immediate stress, and are just as quick to recede. More lasting impressions informing self-organization and the self-other dynamic are formed from the arising of moods, which are the affective undertones that influence our souls. It is the "tunings of mood," especially joy and sadness, that comprise the inner condition of our souls as well as their responses to a subtle influx of moods from others. Alongside the ebb and flow of our moods, which are directly connected to our physical condition, the active and passive movements of the temperaments more profoundly influence our soul life.

The temperaments express the varied colorings of the personality. Steiner uses the ancient tradition of the Four Temperaments—sanguine, choleric, phlegmatic, and melancholic—to illustrate the innate dispositions of reactivity and sensitivity that structure the underlying patterns of our conduct and our attitudes. While every soul is composed of all four temperaments, one of the four is inevitably more prominent in each person. It is the unique configuration of the temperamental tendencies, the way they organize the soul's willing and thinking and relationship to time, that creates the soul's individuality. On a deeper level, because the temperaments express a synthesis "between the things that connect a human being to the ancestral line, and those the human being brings out of earlier incarnations" (1995c, 71), they help us understand the complex relationship between the inherited-physical and the individual-spiritual aspects of the human soul.

With an awareness of the soul processes of emotion, mood, and temperament, we now consider the next sheath in the organization of the self. Imperceptible to the physical eye, the "ether body" is "a subtle body about the same size and shape as the physical body and is composed of an extremely delicate and finely organized structure… [whose] tiny particles are in constant movement. Countless currents stream through it in all directions. These currents maintain and regulate life" (1994, 131–32). While the workings of the formative life-forces of the ether body are independent of our will and consciousness until we engage in esoteric training, it is possible to recognize the way they influence our soul's learning and behavior.

The next member of the human being is the astral body, which manifests itself in different types of character. As a qualitative structure of soul that contains the varieties and vicissitudes of desire, wishes, and longings, the astral body shapes the ambitions and goals of our inner life. Steiner maintains that the essential nature of the astral body is "egoistic," i.e., motivated by "the effort to live solely in and *for* itself" (1997b, 135). There is nothing pejorative in this designation, for Steiner emphasizes that the astral body only manifests *selfish* egoism when it fails to extend its essential self-love toward "universal interests."

The fourth member of the human being, what Steiner calls the ego or "I"-body, only emerges to perception after experience of the astral body creates the feeling that a person's being in the sensory world is *outer* (1997b, 149). While this feeling of existing in the astral body can be "tremendously painful," Steiner remarks that a "second experience" brings to consciousness the knowledge that what was previously taken as our identity is only a mirror of our true nature. This "second experience" consists of a spiritual memory of the divine vision of the cosmic-human as the goal of humanity. It is this "second experience" that allows us both to witness the limitations of normal day-consciousness and to connect with the spiritual beings and realities of the supersensible world.

From the experience of the creative force within this spiritual memory, we come to recognize that we bear the "I"-body deep within our soul.

Let us now apply this awareness of the relationships between the soul's feeling processes and the fourfold embodiment to the "threshold" experience. Remembering that the "threshold" experience challenges the triumph of rationality that has propelled independent self-reflection since the beginning of the modern epoch, we rightly anticipate that human beings will meet the awakening of spiritual awareness with widespread disorientation and skepticism. Furthermore, given that the non-initiatic awakening of spiritual forces occurs as a mostly unconscious yet indisputably felt awareness of danger, the soul is often confronted by experiences that put it into contact with the more shadowy and unacknowledged sides of its personality. To encounter what has previously been denied and disavowed, and to begin to integrate these uninvited and fearful intrusions of spiritual experience, requires the soul to achieve a degree of courage and balance not commonly demonstrated in ordinary consciousness. If the soul fails to attain this maturational leap, it will resort to behaviors that correspond to what psychoanalysis terms disturbances in object relating: extreme and alternating emotional imbalances, the reactivation of immature personality traits, especially anxious and disorganized attachment patterns, and psychic numbing. Consequently, the prevailing form of ego-identity, which is established through standing over and against other beings and nature, cannot conceptualize the arising of spiritual inclusiveness otherwise than as a terrifying disturbance that signals either the diminishment of its freedom and/or the onset of psychosis.

Unprepared to recognize or cross the spiritual "threshold," the soul is traumatized and, recoiling from the shock of transformation, becomes susceptible to obsessions with death and dying. Consequently the soul becomes profoundly devitalized, preoccupied with relentless thoughts and feelings of weakness, enfeeblement, hypochondria, and anhedonia. Hence the life forces are constricted in the physical body, stiffening and twisting the limbic-metabolic systems, and an agitation of the central nervous system creates the impression that the essence of being is continuously disappearing. Chronic fatigue, a syndrome of immobility that totalizes these symptomatic conditions, regardless of whether it is medically diagnosed as an autoimmune deficiency, comes to serve as a metaphor for the condition of the soul's lifelessness.

Connected to but separate from the obsession with death and dying, the soul unprepared for the "threshold" experience becomes pervaded by the fear of an inner fragmenting as well as the terror of falling through a bottomless space. In this traumatized state, the soul agonizes over losing the certainty that the object world and the self, separately or together, are real. When the soul feels groundless, unable to stand on its own two feet or to bear itself, mental functioning devolves into splitting, paranoid distortion, and other pathologically dissociative mechanisms. Engulfed by the sensation of "cracking up" and reduced to utter despair, one becomes subject to out-of-body experiences that lead to oscillations between acute schizoid affectivity and the multiplicity of compartmentalized but partial selves. In its most acute manifestations, the psychological complex appears as an evolving psychotic dispossession of the mind to the point of total annihilation.

The traumatic inner experience of the "threshold" leaves the soul chaotically adrift, unable either to achieve any subjective constancy or to mediate its participation between the physical-corporeal world and the spiritual-moral world. It is as if the radically disconnected soul has been relocated to a dark underground world whose unfamiliar and unearthly terrain overwhelms any attempt at intellectual understanding. Consequently, the soul approaches space-time across the threshold in a self-annihilating mood. Furthermore, unable to offer resistance to this Void by reference to any familiar or objective picture of the self-other-world matrix, the soul becomes attracted to and contracts into the *impulse for delusion*. At this juncture in the "threshold" experience, there arises either the cruel reality of madness, or, even more inwardly, the unavoidable experience of the problem of evil, even to the point where the soul identifies itself as an evil being.

From the vantage point of Steiner's anthroposophical path of modern initiation, it is evident that psychotherapeutic conversation with souls suffering trauma caused by an involuntary "threshold" experience must be oriented toward activating the "I"-body, the *spiritual* "I." As a response to the passivity of the physical body, the disruptions of the rhythms of the etheric body, and the fixations brought about in the astral body, psychotherapeutic activation of the spiritual "I" opens the possibility for free thoughts, warm feelings, and courageous willing that can motivate further meaningful development of the soul. Before offering a more detailed description of some of the features of an anthroposophic psychotherapy, however, let us turn to a non-Freudian psychoanalytic process that engages the traumatic rupturing of the soul by way of an appeal to the world of the spirit.

Torok

In her poetic and artful essay "Theoretra: An Alternative to Theory," M. Torok is concerned with observation of the otherwise passing moment when a verbal, if not always deliberate, expression seizes, in an inescapable awareness, the listener's attention and imagination. While this seizure does not create an actual stoppage of time, it does open the temporal to the eternal. This unexpected moment of interruption, which exposes a previously "segregated" realm of the patient's life, reveals for the therapist an experience that is undigested and possibly indigestible. Being outside symbolization and verbalization, this experience is impossible to integrate into a bearable aspect of the patient's psychic fabric, and immediately abolishes the coherence offered to the therapist by any totalizing theory. Captured by the intensity and novelty of untheorized incoherence, the therapist experiences the momentary rift in the associative train of thought as an invitation to meet the patient's dissociative defense with *wonder*. This pivotal transformation of theory by wonder, precipitated by an untimely and painful awareness of psychic phantoms that apparently arrive from outside of chronological time, is what Torok calls *theoretra*.

To convey the expectations as well as the essence of the *theoretric moment* for psychotherapy, Torok utilizes the archetypal and classical images of the sacred marriage (*hieros gamos*):

Theoretra occurs between the bride and the bridegroom. Both are expecting presents from the other: she will lift her veil, he will hand her gifts. The theoretric moment clinches the pact of a long journey to come, a journey that the brilliance (*theo*) filtering through the uplifted veil serves to announce... (1994, 253)

Torok intuits that the theoretric moment harmonizes the separating differences between the bride and the bridegroom in a brilliance that will hold and join them together from this moment on. (We would offer that the brilliance of this harmony results from the fact that the theoretric arises in the "interfacial region," and that its presence between the unveiling and the offering of gifts symbolizes the encompassing safety afforded by a sacred canopy.) Torok writes that she does not look for the "illumination" that signals the complex appearance of the theoretric moment. When it appears, however, she is prompted to exclaim, with surprise, "there it is, there!" She is further inspired to intone a three-part meditative mantra that not only intensifies the inner experience of promise and hope but also completely reframes the canvas of psychotherapeutic conversation: "Seed of seed. Life of life. Love of love."

Torok informs us that this magical, musical, mystical chant emerges from the unfathomable psychic depths disclosed by the theoretric moment when she, as psychotherapist, surrenders to perceiving, not only within the patient, but also "in between" the two of them, the following traumatic reality:

> He or she is dead. Yet a tiny something survives, emerges from its hiding place. From under the veil, he or she lets me catch a glimpse, hear a whisper of some continuing faint movement or noise. There is a murmur, a ventriloquy, rising from the tomb in which he or she or someone else, either a contemporary or an ancestor, was buried alive, sequestered, with their desires cut out, deprived of both life and death. (Ibid., 254)

For Torok, it does not matter how long this psycho-physical trauma has been encrypted in the patient's personal history. What is important is that the theoretric event is always revelatory. As the initial vulnerability produced by this "glimpse" of something hidden matures into an inner experience in and between both participants, the encounter becomes qualitatively enlivened and the psychotherapeutic conversation transforms the feeling of entrapment in a place of entombment into the security that arises from a place for incubation. Regenerating the psychotherapeutic processes and redirecting our understanding of trauma, theoretra is "a welcoming acceptance, an entrance."

Taking a "cryptological plunge" that inaugurates a joint conjuring of dead voices in the hopes of reviving hovering ghosts, Torok shifts the discursive logic of psychoananlysis in a way that affirms the potential creativity of dissociation: "in the theoretric moment there is trance." That is, the "entrance" that opens the psychotherapeutic conversation to extend hospitality to the previously unspeakable, because unconscionable, pain of trauma is trance: "Right there, the two partners will on occasion fall asleep together, dream the same word, the same image, for an instant, and for once have a real session...."

Clearly conscious that she is challenging the rationalist presuppositions that define psychoanalysis as a modern science, Torok calls this "real session, séance." By linking the psychoanalytic approach to the theoretric moment, and by stipulating that the thoeretric moment contains trance as the "trance-formative" force that leads the session to become a séance, Torok reveals that psychotherapeutic conversation with sufferers of traumatic pain requires a practice that goes beyond both the exclusive use of language and the cultivation of empathy.

According to Torok, if psychotherapy with traumatic pain is to open to the possible renewal of a life once extinguished, then it must be prepared "to summon the specter, the spirit of the spirit of Spirit itself, assassinated by some ghost." As a new form of practice with traumatic pain, the séance, a term Torok appropriates from the type of meeting where people sit together with a spiritualist in the hope of receiving messages from those who have passed beyond the living, enacts the theoretric event where "like attracts like" in order to extract the "difficult from the difficult." Beyond giving hospitality to the ghosts and spirits that the patient has inherited from the "contemporary or ancestral" branches of his or her physical life, the séance opens the experience of the unconscious from a search for logic to the play of imagination. Fortifying her resistance to an exclusively analytic approach for psychotherapeutic conversation, Torok further asserts that the "theoretric moment is always preceded by a long series of séances."

Torok maintains that this long psychotherapeutic apprenticeship in mediumship is necessary because the "absent spirits arrive not so much through invocation as through a convoking summons." While we can speculate that the failure of many psychotherapists to assume the role of "summoner of the spirits" results from either their unwillingness to relinquish the privilege of power that allows for a covert control of the psychotherapeutic conversation or their disdain for the reality of the occult, Torok is quite clear about the human attributes desired by the absent spirits in the work of healing traumatic pain. In addition to the embodiment of compassion, she specifies that it is crucial for the therapist to surrender all preconceptions concerning the pathology of dissociation: "For them to rap, for them to want to rap, the spirits need to understand that their absence has always already been a presence in the form of unrecognized knowledge, a nescience. They must understand that we were able to surmise this."

Reading Torok's description of the desire of the spirits, it is incumbent [upon us] to ask, "How do the spirits surmise that the partners in the psychotherapeutic conversation have overcome the affective and cognitive denials contained in the reality of the patient's trauma?" Appropriating Torok's suggestions, it seems to us that the spirits' desire to "rap" is immediately gratified by the therapist's attaining the capacity to trance. It also seems that the therapist's trance-gressive exit from the role of the one who is "supposed to know" is required if the spirits' "need to be understood" is to be fulfilled. Furthermore, it seems that the therapist's willingness to act as a medium and to allow the psychotherapeutic conversation to trance-form itself into a séance that wholeheartedly "summons" the absent spirits is the encouragement they need to rap the songs that unwrap the truths concealed in the symptoms of trauma. From these considerations concerning the performative affirmation of séance, which only takes place in the "interfacial region," psychotherapeutic conversation can more securely hold the patient's experience of traumatic pain and can begin to decipher the dissociative strategies that encrypt the soul's isolation, polarization, and fragmentation.

Anthroposophic Psychotherapy

Our discussion of psychotherapeutic conversation has been guided by Steiner's observation of a transition in consciousness that will enhance the naturally evolving development of clairvoyant faculties. Beyond unformulated and uncanny experiences that reveal the limitations both of knowledge gained from sense perception of the physical world and of analysis of the subconscious, this evolution of consciousness will reveal the reality of the etheric body. While this revelation will be overwhelming and traumatic, those who deny it out of a continued loyalty to a materialistic conception of reality will have to confront feelings of madness.

If the practice of psychotherapeutic conversation is to offer true healing from the trauma of a "threshold" experience, therapists must be prepared to encounter souls exhibiting behavioral-relational dynamics dominated by "bizarre objects" (Bion 1983), encapsulated partial-selves, emotional symptoms that cluster around real and illusory threats of violence, and mental functioning characterized by a tendency toward pathological dissociation. More directly, psychotherapeutic conversation with traumatized patients means being present with souls who live more or less unconsciously in psychic structures that are permeated by *emptiness* and in affect states that are characterized by *blankness*. Given that trauma arrests the continuous development of the soul, freezing its "becoming" and "beginning" aspirations in abstract conceptualizations taken over from collective structures of consciousness, true healing requires therapists to provide emotional mirroring, to offer the corrective insight necessary to reconstruct the past, and to be willing to summon the astral spirits. Additionally, the healthy transformation of souls that have been shattered by the overpowering experience of the "threshold" requires therapists to enter and utilize the "interfacial region" of relating and communicating as a medium for the creation of a path of inner development that is animated by the spiritual "I."

In distinction to the ego of everyday consciousness, which is achieved through identifying with fixed contents derived from past consciousness, the spiritual "I" is a living, primal being that is always in development. The spiritual "I" is without predicates; it is not who I *could* or *should* be, not *this* or *that* role I play or position I have attained. The spiritual "I" is not even the feelings I have about myself, which are only the result of energies that may or may not be liberated from subconscious impulses that take the form of self-assertions and self-denials. Shorn of all these ideas and representational identities, the spiritual "I" supports itself on nothing; it is no-thing, except that it is; it simply is who "**I am.**"

To transform psychotherapeutic conversation from a practice concerned with pathologies of the ego and its relations with the object world, which primarily shows us who we are *not*, to an involvement with processes centered on the influence of the spiritual "I," calls for an education of the soul that Steiner associates with *initiation*. While initiation rites in all cultures throughout history have been designed to awaken the soul to higher stages of consciousness and to provide the means of healing physical and emotional maladies, traditionally initiation was restricted to only those chosen by tribal elders or priests. Psychotherapeutic initiation, on the other hand, especially with patients suffering the debilitating effects of the terrifying destructiveness that increasingly confronts all of us living in the modern epoch, is an everyday rite of passage. Rather than preoccupying itself with how the sacred mysteries of birth, death, and resurrection find expression in the realm of the profane, modern psychotherapeutic initiation aims to extricate the self from attachments to habitual thoughts and behaviors, and to increase the possibilities for autonomy and authenticity that allow us to experience ourselves in the vibrancy and vitality of the present moment. Recognizing that the already-constituted psycho-cultural beliefs, motivations, and narcissistic investments that compose the ordinary ego no longer offer sufficient sustenance for constructing a meaningful and purposeful life, modern psychotherapeutic intiation turns our quest to a healing that entails peace and justice, and directs us toward the spiritual "I." Bringing us into contact with the time stream from the future, where the self and the world are both unformed and awaiting our most creative and compassionate efforts, initiation, through encountering the love and wisdom of the spiritual "I," can teach our souls to trust the unknown.

We have mentioned that anthroposophic psychotherapy, in addition to resolving conflicts that arise from characterological disorders and addressing relationship impasses that result from temperament incompatibilities, is a path of inner training. Assuming that psychotherapeutic conversation were to assimilate this initiatic orientation, especially with those suffering the trauma of physical and emotional violence as well as precocious spiritual development, we can see that therapists must go beyond even empathic and non-judgmental participation in the "interfacial region" of relationship and communication. Unavoidably, therapists must themselves experience how the path of consciousness education is an *inner* path on the way to the spiritual "I." To become soul healers and guides in the further consciousness expansion of their patients, therapists working on their own inner path would be well advised to adopt practices specifically designed to deepen the resilience of the soul and to enhance the possibility of achieving spiritual knowledge. Drawing from the wealth of examples provided by Steiner (2005), I would suggest the following preparatory exercises: taking moments for inner stillness; intense observation of the natural and social world; impartial observation of one's own actions and non-judgment toward other people; tolerance of others' viewpoints; seeking the positive in the self and others; feeling gratitude for what the world and others have given; cultivating equanimity of feeling.

In addition to these observational exercises, which aim at refining the soul and nurturing its cognitive faculties, Steiner stipulates undertaking the following six "supplementary" practices (1994a):

Control of thinking
Control of action (will)
Control of feeling (equanimity)
Impartiality (open-mindedness)
Trust (openness toward life)
Inner harmony

As steps on the inner path, all of these exercises and practices contribute to overcoming the deeply ingrained reactive approach-avoidance tendencies that leave us prey to psychic distractions and epistemological distortions. On the more profound level of supporting the development of concentrated attention, the prerequisite for attaining spiritual knowledge, the exercises and practices serve to cultivate an appreciation for the activity that defines Steiner's teaching: *meditation*.

Prior to an intensive immersion and repetitive absorption in a content or image, Steiner's meditation approach, which eschews the traditional Eastern emphasis on breath regulation, cultivates the seeker's capacity for tolerating the experience of silence. Undertaken in full awareness, meditative silence is less the absence of noise, the suspension of the voice, or the cessation of language than the illuminating presence of inner stillness. Meditative silence furthers the inner path of awakening from the concerns of the everyday self, which substitutes the purposes of practical life for the meanings of human existence. As distinct from the dead silence produced by nihilistic terror, in which we realize the inadequacy and unreliability of ordinary experience to account for the reality that is beyond it, meditative silence dissolves the obscuring fantasies that separate inside and outside, permanence and impermanence, subject and object, and ourselves and the world. Cultivating a moment-to-moment attention that allows us to cut through organized habits, inertia, and segmenting and sharply defined boundaries, meditative silence opens up a horizon where experiences inherently and spontaneously arise and a field of non-judgmental and mutual interpenetration allows us to face reality as it is.

Abiding in the pure manifestation of reality, meditative silence enables the transition from the inauthentic censorings imposed by ego-centeredness to the authentic sense of inclusiveness that characterizes the spiritual "I." The integrity of this state of inclusiveness, which is beyond the pleasure of any self-improvement or self-empowerment, is revealed by the way meditative silence gives access to the inner creative and moral forces of the "I" and awakens the *centering heart* as an organ of perception (Sardello 2006). Animated by the capacity for play, wonder, and selflessness, the centering heart engenders a new form of knowing whose source is the ever-present origin of living presence. Meditatively dwelling in this light-filled heart-centeredness, detached from the anxieties associated with justification and performance, the "I" is granted the preparedness and readiness necessary to receive the gift of imaginative cognitions. The interior, meditative process of working with these heart-centered imaginative cognitions, which are the first sign of modern clairvoyance, opens the "I" to the awareness that it lives its essential aloneness always at one with others in a unified and qualitative world. Providing an impetus to venture beyond already acquired and confining systems of meaning, meditative deepening of imaginative cognition and engaging in formative action permits the "I" to attain the intuitive certainty that life is inseparable from intrinsic freedom.

As therapists struggle to understand patients suffering from the dehumanizing violations and violence that result in trauma, can anything less than the realization of this stage of meditatively attained imaginative consciousness be their goal?

Conclusion

Steiner was acutely aware that crossing the "threshold" to perception of the spiritual world, which occurs more and more frequently in our time, represents an evolution of consciousness that most souls will find traumatic. To counter the fear and suffering provoked by this now unavoidable journey, Steiner offered researches into the unconscious that both include and transcend the discoveries of psychoanalysis. In addition to locating subconscious forces hitherto rejected by an egoity incarcerated in the fear and self-loathing that arise from conforming to materialist ideologies, Steiner's spiritual science offers an understanding of the human soul that frees us from the determinisms of instinctual and hereditary conditioning, thereby rescuing us from the annihilation of soullessness.

From his multidimensional portrait of the unconscious, Steiner also identifies a supersensible dimension populated with spiritual beings and realities. To reduce the risk of pathological dissociation that can accompany an unprepared crossing of the "threshold" to the spiritual world, and to facilitate the "threshold" experience as a deed of freedom, Steiner teaches an inner path of development that cultivates the enlivening of thinking, feeling, and willing. On a deeper level, Steiner's way of self-knowledge intends to establish an intimate human-earthly relation between soul wisdom and cosmic love, and to contribute to the development of modern clairvoyant faculties. If this fundamental curative effort for the health of the soul and the earth is to fulfill its aim at this time of universalized terror, then psychotherapeutic conversation can no longer settle for improvements in technique and theory that at best modify behavior and at worst deaden imagination, but must partake in the leap of consciousness necessary to awaken initiatic consciousness.

Chapter 5

PSYCHOTHERAPY AS A VOCATION:
GIVING VOICE TO SOUL

W E COULD HARDLY expect the universalization of terror, contaminating as it does all relationships in the modern epoch, to spare the vocation of psychotherapy. Terror threatens the soul and its freedom, not only in the increasing prevalence of post-traumatic stress disorder, but also in the way restrictive legislative policies, the constriction of insurance benefits, and the quick fixes of guru-like media "shrinks" reduce the psychotherapeutic work of diagnosing and ameliorating individual, marital, and family dysfunctions to little more than the application of behavioral techniques designed to repair personality disorders. In addition, the widespread influence of psychopharmacology, which first postulates a neurobiological source for emotional-mental suffering and then produces medications aimed at symptom relief, erodes the appreciation of and the desire to understand the complexity of the dynamic unconscious. Disinclined to pursue a holistic conception of the unconscious or to value a deliberate and intentional resolution of unconscious psychic conflict—negations that reflect a deeper indifference to the quest for existential wisdom—the materialistic approaches of behaviorism and biologism prevent psychotherapy from becoming a calling that facilitates either a true inner journey of discovery or a profoundly creative inter/trans-subjective encounter. To overcome these impediments to the actualization of new knowledge, truly transformative healing, and the maturity necessary to participate in just, respectful, and intimate relationships, this chapter will offer a portrait of the psychotherapeutic encounter as an engagement between the dynamic unconscious and soul life. While respectful of the analytic tradition of thinking about the unconscious, our picture of this encounter will emphasize Rudolf Steiner's researches into the dynamics of the human relation, which reveal our soul life to be invested with a spiritual element whose appreciation and cultivation can help us to welcome the unknown aspects of our destiny.

It is obvious that social forces are imposing economic and epistemologic constraints to frustrate the psychotherapeutic process from becoming a path where the wordless knowledge within the word can come to linguistic expression and embrace the essential embodied spirituality of the human soul. Nevertheless, if psychotherapy is to fulfill its vocational call and eventuate in a true and truthful "talking cure," it must respond to the unconscionable ways that violent terror obliterates a healthy concern for the fragility of life and renders the soul mute. Faced with caring for souls whose sense of well-being has been severely compromised, if not destroyed, by experiences of which they cannot speak, the work of psychotherapy must become a way of giving voice to states of being that seem unrepresentable. By infusing the dyadic enactment between free association and attentive listening with a deep respect for the ever-present mystery of otherness—both the finite other and the infinite Other—psychotherapy can become an ethical practice that enables souls to develop the capacities necessary to confront the barbarism that defines our epoch.

If psychotherapy is to explore the intensities and dimensions of the dynamic unconscious, it is not enough to limit our analytic inquiry to the vicissitudes of the will to power. Obviously, psychotherapy must continue to occupy itself with the domain of self-sentient emotional life, especially with the suffering caused by the fact that the feeling and willing elements of soul life escape conscious cognition. For the most part, however, psychotherapy has restricted its pursuit of the unknown to an exploration of the subconscious. Past the border of everyday consciousness, the subconscious is composed of unrefined energies and unmetabolized impulses of personality fragments. Understandable as an effective force of non-cognizing that gives shape to incomprehensible emotions, the subconscious operates under the direction of an unrepentant and ruthless egoism. The negative "effects" it emits in such "irrational" formations, e.g., symptoms and complexes, give rise to the habits and structures of mind that inhibit the development of autonomous thinking and perceiving. Since the precognitive, nefarious, and pre-linguistic activities of these subconscious "effects" prevent the soul from engaging others and the world with compassion and love, psychotherapy is called upon to undertake and become identified with symbolic processes that require interpretation.

Regardless of how well interpretation names and manages the disturbances produced by the "effects" of the subconscious, and how crucial are its successes to the amelioration of emotional suffering and relational dysfunction, the psychotherapeutic experience of the unconscious is incomplete as long as it fails to recognize the reality of the *supraconscious*. Across the upper boundary of everyday consciousness, the supraconscious is that area of the unconscious that "contains the *possibility of all forms*, qualities and conceptualities" (Kühlewind 1990, 65). Characterized by potentiality, which is the condition of the soul's freedom, the supraconscious is the realm of pure abilities, of capacities whose formative essences remain unfinished and whose dynamic thrust is ruled by the play of improvisation. As distinct from the subconscious area of the unconscious, which pre-shapes privatized, idiosyncratic, and egocentric forms of soul life according to patterns of self-feeling derived from past experiences, the supraconscious is defined by a quality of unified wholeness that consists of the creative capacities conducive to individuation, the possibility for undistorted communication, and, as a prelude to intuitive thinking, the shaping of new thoughts. As the creative source of the formative movement through which psychological phenomena such as archetypes and complexes coalesce and eventually incarnate, thereby engendering the soul's possibilities for self-awareness, the supraconscious enfolds and unfolds universal abilities. As described by Georg Kühlewind, "the possibilities of creating forms come from the other side; they are spiritual abilities. They come from a world, the world of the spirit, that cannot at first be consciously experienced by man" (1988, 33).

Note the important qualification contained in Kühlewind's statement: the supraconscious, which originates in the invisible "world of the spirit" and contains the spiritual abilities that awaken intuitions of "I-consciousness and I-experience," cannot be consciously experienced by human beings "at first." Primarily, this caveat corrects the error whereby the social sciences, inclusive of self and relational psychology, reduce the supraconscious to a subjective feeling best relegated to the realm of religion. Kühlewind also provides a hint here, which his teachings certainly bear out: that human beings can attain the capacity to consciously perceive and cognize the spiritual world.

To facilitate greater proximity to this new stage of consciousness and type of knowledge, whose possibility is announced with the simultaneous opening of the spiritual world to conscious experience and the opening of consciousness to the invisible emanations from the spiritual world, psychotherapy must expand its interpretive practice. If it is to attain the continuity of understanding and realize the possibilities of authenticity and individuation it values, psychotherapy must participate in a leap of thinking that turns toward the supraconscious unknown, and thus surrender its obsession with resolving the transference.

Understood by psychotherapy as it applies to work with the subconscious, the transference refers to the erotic connection between the patient and the therapist that functions as a substitute for the presence of someone from the past, most notably the father, the mother, or some archetypal figure. The activation of this affective intersubjectivity through the unique and provisional care quality of the psychotherapeutic relationship unleashes an onslaught of subconscious energies, bringing the most intense of previously unremembered emotional experiences, both painful losses and rapturous attachments, into language. Since it is this activation that uncovers the "truth" of a damaged life, recognition of the transference often becomes the object of therapeutic treatment. When this fascination with the transference relationship does occur, then the danger is that the adored/resented transferential object will be perceived as forever available yet unattainable. As an affective repetition of the enigmatic parent-child dynamic, the transference, fully saturated with passions, thwarts interpretive closure and challenges the termination of therapy, whose measure of success is separation without annihilation.

Another reason for psychotherapy to expand the range of its interpretive practice is that crossing the threshold to the supraconscious eventuates a new form of transference. If we recognize that this ascent in consciousness involves a transition to a world whose "unknown" factor is not the repressed or dissociated "what has been" but rather an awe-inspiring mystery whose emergence is "what will be," we will conclude that interpretive psychotherapeutic work must move beyond the intellectualized explanation of the "effects" of past conditioning. In this exhilarating and anxiety-ridden encounter with spiritual beings and forces whose undeniable reality has no precedence in the patient's experience, the interpretive work of psychotherapy rests entirely upon the therapist's embodiment of unconditional presence. Irreducible to any strategy or technique, it is the unassuming but all-embracing quality of the therapist's presence that opens psychotherapeutic work to a nonjudgmental, reciprocal, and mutually respectful inquiry into the heights and depths of human experience. Permeated by a moral imagination that attests to the therapist's "living within" rather than "talking about" the cauldron of suffering and compassion, it is the luminous and radiating presence of wisdom and love that allows the interpretive work of psychotherapy to unfold in the direction of the unknown supraconscious, such that the life of the soul becomes oriented to uniting with the eternal truth of its spiritual origins.

To build a bridge between the interpretive healing of subconscious trauma and the therapeutic work that takes psychological problems as providing specific types of opportunity for supraconscious experience and the becoming of our spirit self, let us refer to the work of W. R. Bion. Among Bion's most salient theoretic contributions to establishing the "mystical" aspects of psychotherapy is his phenomenological reformulation of the relationship between observation and temporality. Building upon Freud's stipulation that the analyst should attain "freely hovering" attention (1983), Bion conceives the analytic session as an experience that is concerned neither with any history or future, nor with sense impressions or objects. Rather, what is of interest in the analytic session is only the psychic reality of "what is happening" (1992, 380). What Bion discovers in this "happening" is that the temporality of the session is invested with a timelessness that both cuts *across* time itself and originates the new moment that permits the *coming-up* of the instant of surprise. Furthermore, by offering unprejudiced attention to whatever arises in the instant of surprise, whether the event is catastrophic or ecstatic, the analyst can remain open to the fact that "the only point of importance in any session is the unknown" (Ibid., 381).

By reorienting the purpose of the session from the uncovering of repressed subconscious material to the emergence of new thoughts from the analysand's unknown, Bion transforms psychoanalysis from a positivistic science of consciousness to an exploration of the "dark and formless infinite" of the psyche (Grotstein 1995). To facilitate this process of opening to the supraconscious source of ideas, which parallels the mystic's soul-searching journey for Truth, the analyst's attention must attain a degree of discipline that is analogous to an "act of faith" (1970, 32). For Bion, the rules of this sacramental discipline are simple: "denial of memory, desire and understanding" (Ibid., 41–53). This denial of what Bion calls "opacities" (1992, 315) that block the heightening of attention is not to be confused with negating the analyst's process of cognition. Rather, this inhibition or sacrifice of the sensuous elements in thinking is necessary if the analyst is to gain access to the inwardly receptive sense organ of intuition.

For Bion, intuition is more than a mode of thinking. Intuition is also a mode of relating and communicating that permits investigation of the ineffable matrix of the psyche that Bion calls "O" (1965). As his expression for the Ultimate Reality that already always "*is*," existing both before and after the working of the drives, sense-perception, imagination, and conceptualization, "O" is the Transcendent Other, the cosmic domain both eternally near and forever distant from the ordinary reality we take for granted. Beyond the order of being through which the psyche represents its affective identifications and encumbrances to itself and others, "O" is approachable only through an intuitive attention that is empty of predeterminations and is able to engage in "contemplation without an object to contemplate" (Grotstein 1995).

Bion's understanding of how intuition allows for transformations in "O" is evident in his conception of the "container/contained" (1970). The containing mother must accept her infant's projected fears, especially of dying, and, through her reverie function (an intuitional process of absorption, purification, and translation) evolve distress into acceptable meaning. From his insight into this primal scene, where not only psychic survival but also maturation depends upon the intuitively resonant relation between both parties, Bion can suggest that the "happening" of the analytic session follows a three-part movement. First, as the attention of the therapist becomes increasingly intuitive, which presupposes the arduous and painful overcoming of persecutory and depressive anxieties, the container for the patient's dread of the unknown becomes increasingly attuned and receptive. Second, as the patient feels less scrutinized for faults and more empathically-intuitively received, he or she is able to participate with "less clogging of the sessions by the repetition of material that should have disappeared" (1992, 382). Third, as both the therapist and the patient can now more readily enter the analytic situation as a "happening" of self-awareness without reference to objects and object relations, there occurs a greater possibility for intuitions of the unknown to emerge as a realization of conflict-free Truth.

When the analytic session "happens" as a cycle of transformations in and between both participants' intuitions of the presence of the awesome unknownness of Truth—which reflects both parties having achieved the capacities for mourning, reparation, tolerance of ambivalence, and selfless love—there "happens" the psychic enlightenment where the attainment of peace with oneself and the other corresponds to an abiding-becoming in communion with "O."

Toward an Anthroposophic Psychotherapy

While psychotherapy held little interest for Steiner, except insofar as it infiltrated and rivaled the work of Anthroposophy, he regarded the unprecedented character of the modern human encounter as crucial. Whether consideration of the human encounter relates to his program for social renewal (1941), appears as an aspect of his theory of evolution

(1997a), or is included in the reverse ritual as a stage in community formation (2001), Steiner emphasizes that "we must permeate ourselves deeply with the consciousness that in this epoch for the first time human ego meets human ego in an intercourse of soul that is free of all veils" (1987, 152). This freedom derives from the historical transformation whereby human encounters, "soul intercourse," take place less within the diminishing force of instinctual or blood-based relationships and increasingly within the ascending force of the individual element. This unraveling of associations ruled by blood affinity and their replacement by encounters between free individuals opens social relations to the potential conscious realization of what Steiner calls "elective affinity" (1941, 177). Yet the transcendence of group participation, which is essential for the complete unfolding of the personality, has had the side-effect of establishing an unlimited personal egoism, which more often than not results in a mutual lack of interest, and the neglecting and objectifying of human beings by one another.

Steiner's invective against this interpersonal indifference, which manifests a general non-relation to every other human being, reflects his awareness that social problems cannot be resolved without knowledge of the essence of the human being. In his important lecture "Social and Antisocial Forces" (1941), given as part of his consideration of the threefold social organization, Steiner offers a consideration of how the human soul, in its aspects of thinking, feeling, and willing, manifests itself in social relationships. Speaking of these soul activities from the standpoint of their subconscious workings, thereby locating the source of their antisocial tendency, this lecture allows us to consider the human encounter from the perspective of the tasks awaiting the initiation of a spiritual psychology.

As an interaction between separate individuals, the face-to-face encounter oscillates between the extreme alternatives of submerged belonging and isolated loneliness. Emphasizing that both tendencies, the social as well as the antisocial, are at work in each of the soul-faculties during every meeting between two human beings, Steiner contends that the basic social dynamic, albeit on a subconscious level, consists of a process whereby "one person is always trying to put the other to sleep, while the other is trying to stay awake" (Ibid., 124). Insofar as the basic phenomenology of the encounter is perceived as an intrusion of foreignness that is synonymous with the threat of attack, the soul-forces of the Self, which in our time are oriented toward self-expression and the satisfaction of our needs rather than toward self-restraint and compassion, lurch toward the antisocial impulse. With the ascent of the antisocial tendency, which is inevitable given our epoch's affirmation of unfettered independence and dread of codependence, the human encounter becomes indistinguishable from an act of confrontation whereby the other becomes reduced to either an opportunity for or an impediment to self-realization. As a consequence of displacing/replacing the implicit civility of human encounters with mechanisms of exchange, social life becomes patterned on an economic model totally committed to profit and loss.

Let us look at how the antisocial instinct affects the forces of the soul. The prevalence of the antisocial instinct in thinking gives rise to a conceptual life that is self-referential. Self-protective in the face of the other's sleep-inducing powers, the self encloses itself in the content of its own thoughts. According little or no value to the other's thoughts, one rarely attempts to suppress one's incessant inner chatter and truly listen. One may seize upon something the other says as a pretext for restating one's own views, frequently from a position of criticism and contempt for the other. In these antisocial dynamics, thinking is utilized as a way to enhance self-experiencing, and as an intellectual defense employed to maintain identity, inhibit communication, and preclude thoughtful relations with the other.

The human soul is a being of feeling as well as of thinking. In the feeling realm of the soul, sympathies and antipathies constantly vibrate in a natural judging process that Steiner understands to "always sketch a false picture of the other person" (Ibid., 132). As a result of this natural falsifying tendency in the feeling realm of the soul, which is predicated upon the subjective basis of likes and dislikes, the human encounter is prey to either overestimation or devaluation by each person in the relationship. Structured by these antisocial impulses, the human encounter is enacted as an arhythmic movement between emotional extremes, such as fascination, which elicits the urge to merge, and repulsion, which provokes the urge to withdraw. Regardless of which feeling predominates—and the variety of emotional polarities is extensive—projections and associations whose source remains hidden and whose appearance imperils self-identity, riddle the entire interaction. Consequently, rather than becoming an opportunity for empathic contact that would allow both people to get to know and appreciate each other, the human encounter deteriorates into a power struggle laden with the antipathies of anger, blame, and fear.

Steiner is acutely aware that examination of the subconscious play between sympathy and antipathy is antagonistic to most people. Averse to honest introspection and lacking the devotion necessary to attain self-knowledge, most people go through life confused about or in a dreamy relation to their feelings. As a result of this tendency toward ordinary complacency, most people are prone to exaggerate or lose themselves in encounters with others. And nowhere is the tendency toward self-delusion and self-abdication more pronounced than when it relates to the feeling of love. In fact, Steiner claims "that the love manifesting itself between one person and another…is not really love as such, but an image the person makes of love…in the great majority of cases the love that plays its role between people and is called love is only masked egoism, the source of the greatest imaginable and most widespread antisocial impulse" (Ibid., 135–36). From this egocentric misconception regarding the feeling of love, whose violence is evident in such behaviors as the use of sarcasm, the lack of tenderness toward the vulnerability of the other, and the need to hurt the other if our unwarranted sense of entitlement and desire for adoration are unfulfilled, the antisocial instinct prevents the human encounter from becoming both a source of healing and a path on the way toward living with and into the mystery of intimacy.

As it pertains to the soul faculty of willing, which relates to the sphere of activity and reactivity, the workings of the antisocial instinct in the feeling of love have a particularly insidious influence. Steiner is quite direct here: "For everything that envelops all relationships in will between people must be viewed in the light of the impelling force that underlies these volitional relationships, that is, in the light of the love that plays its role in greater or lesser degree" (Ibid., 134). Propelled by an egocentric feeling of love that is largely illusory and only rarely embraces the essential reality of the other, the human encounter becomes a field of activity dominated by the forces of expansion and contraction. More specifically, the antisocial aspect of the will contributes to an inflated sense of self-importance where all that matters is "what's in it for me?" Always utilizing the human encounter to the detriment and diminishment of the other, the overly willful self operates through manipulative strategies such as gaining the advantage, securing the upper hand, and controlling the high ground. Regardless of the behavior, the goal of the antisocial will-driven soul is always the same: to overwhelm if not destroy the separateness of the other.

In its most extreme form, the antisocial tendency of the will leads to abusive encounters. When the subconscious will-forces of the soul activate behaviors that pervert the flowering of sublime joy and selfless devotion, pleasure is derived from domination, subjugation and the infliction of humiliation. To the person motivated by fear and hatred (which are often hidden under the veneer of strength and superiority), the very existence of the other becomes a pretext for the soul-forces of the will to engage in violent aggression. Under these conditions, it is impossible for the encounter between human beings to yield a deeply loving relationship. Instead, the human encounter becomes an altercation where the unleashing of power occasions only unbearable anguish and unmediated wounding. Inseparable from the profanity of terror, the human encounter exposes the subjectivity of the other to an invasion whose inhumanity is so radically hostile that the soul, if not annihilated, is rendered autistic.

If psychotherapy is to contribute to softening the antisocial instinct that excludes from the human encounter all sense of responsibility for the other, it must free individuals from their obsessive attachment to the vicissitudes of self-love. To accomplish the difficult task of healing egocentric auto-affection, whose pernicious aims are not limited to projects of aggrandizement but always include the dehumanization of the other, psychotherapy must detach from the tendency to align itself with the presuppositions of materialist science or with the prejudices of social work. Additionally, for psychotherapy to become a truly creative discipline that is attuned to the mystery of human relations, it must avoid getting lost in the depths of the subconscious. Resisting the lures of these detours, psychotherapy can become a guardian of the space of possibility wherein the human encounter can remain susceptible to the gentle call of the Spirit. By responding to the call to cultivate knowledge of the supraconscious, psychotherapy becomes a practice whereby the desire at work in human relations does not incorporate the other's being in mine or dissolve me in the other's being. At issue here is neither dialectical unity nor mystical fusion. Rather, in the service of opening the soul to the light of the Spirit, psychotherapy promotes a self-integration capable of both rejecting the security of egoic totality and accepting, without hesitation, an infinite responsibility for the other.

In calling for psychotherapy to nurture the spiritual dimension of existence, we are not suggesting that it avoid confronting the psychological and social traumas that characterize contemporary existence. Rather, from an awareness of the superconscious, we ask that psychotherapy begins to speak a "*logos* of the soul" that includes an understanding that spiritual beings and realities are working both positively and negatively into material life. Consequently, we are concerned that the "logic" animating psychotherapy orient soul wisdom to balance "those forces that oppose harmonizing humanity as a whole" (Ibid., 153). Assimilating Steiner, if we are going to perceive the influences of the spiritual worlds upon psychotherapy, and upon the larger questions of social organization, we cannot omit further consideration of the Luciferic and Ahrimanic beings (1993). These spiritual figures are so significant, in fact, that consideration of Lucifer and Ahriman in their opposing roles, mediated by humanity and its sense of the Divine, results in the realization that both world and human evolution can really be understood only "from the point of view of a trinity" (1941, 154).

In Steiner's lecture cycle *The Mission of the Archangel Michael*, we find a multidimensional commentary on the workings of Lucifer and Ahriman. One way of understanding his approach is by way of a triadic analogy to what can be called "soul anatomy." By paralleling the soul-faculties of thinking, feeling, and willing to the physiology of the nervous system, the rhythmic organization, and the limbic-metabolic system, Steiner locates the working of Lucifer above and Ahriman below. Luciferic spirituality is involved with the intellect, with the function and structure of the head, with visionary experience, with the mistaking of fantasy for reality, and with the striving for a universal freedom that would make human beings "unfaithful...to forsake their divine creator-beings" (1994b, 104). Luciferic emotionality tends toward the aerial; inflation, elation, mania, and lack of interest in other people. Ahrimanic spirituality, on the other hand, is involved with the vitality of the will, with digestion and movement, with desires that bind humanity to the physical realm of the body and the materiality of the earth, and with the substitution of an adherence to collective goals instead of an individual pursuit of ethical-divine ideals. Ahrimanic emotionality tends toward the terrestial; depression, despair, the domination of others, and the striving "to draw humanity and everything connected with it into [its] power...lasting dominion" (Ibid.).

From these cursory descriptions we can surmise how the Luciferic and Ahrimanic impulses work to increase the antisocial or pathological element both within the individual soul and between souls in relationship (1993). We can also begin to imagine what our possession by these spiritual beings implies for a psychotherapy that would be a "*logos* of the soul.*" When an individual soul is under the sway of Luciferic "head" thinking, the intellect is accorded the privilege of establishing the quality of truth and determining the hierarchy of values. This "head" thinking results in the one-sidedness of abstraction, and motivates us to find validation in self-absorption and objectification. From this rarefied and reified form of living, which is ultimately comfort-seeking, the human encounter devolves toward the avoidance of deadness, and the other is used both to satisfy the need for self-aggrandizement and to fulfill the role of a sacrificial victim. When an individual soul is under the sway of the Ahrimanic will to power, actions are accorded the privilege of establishing the distribution of rights, and ends are used to justify the means. The result of this one-sidedness is an obsession with might that leads toward constant self-fortification and humiliation. From this competitive and antagonistic way of living, which is ultimately driven by anticipatory anxiety, the human encounter is oriented toward the perpetuation of control, and the other is used both to satisfy the need for internal security and to fulfill the role of a demonized enemy.

In addition to absorbing these pictures into the work of psychotherapy, it is important to remember that the soul's task of balancing the Luciferic captivation of intelligence and the Ahrimanic appropriation of the will has, since 1879, taken place under the spiritual guidance of the Archangel Michael. The mission of Michael, who is known as the "Countenance of God" (Ibid., 44), is inseparable from the eternal human quest for a genuine knowledge of the Divine that would reveal the true secrets of human nature as well as the significance of our connection to the earth. In the ancient Hebraic culture, this revelation occurred as the passive yet clairvoyant reception of Michael's transmission of the word of God in night-dreams. Because of the Mystery of Golgotha, however, wherein the Christ-Being lived in a human body and passed through death, "human beings acquired the possibility of cognizing the divine creative powers not only during sleep but in ordinary waking day-consciousness as well" (Ibid., 122). As a consequence of this unprecedented and unrepeatable historical-spiritual event, Michael, once the revealer by night, now must become the revealer by day. An important implication of this aspect of the contemporary mission of Michael, whose balancing of the adversarial influences of Lucifer and Ahriman takes place during the evolutionary epoch of developing freedom that began with the end of the Kali Yuga (1899), is that spiritual assistance is less a bequest by the hierarchies than the result of active participation by individuals in the quest for higher consciousness.

To counter the Luciferic tendency toward abstraction and emotionality and the Ahrimanic tendency to gravitate toward and obey the strongest authoritarian will, as well as to facilitate the contemporary Michael revelation, which has to do with overcoming evil and death, psychotherapy is called upon to imbue individuals and human encounters with a vividly felt soul-reality of the spiritual in our immediate earthly environment. If psychotherapy is to contribute to this awareness, it must prepare us to realize that the antisocial and egoistic powers of Lucifer and Ahriman can only unfold through a combination of our neglect and their theft of our own highest creative forces. Upon our attainment of this awareness and insight, psychotherapy can contribute to the initiation of another, unknown destiny by freely transforming itself into a "schooling of consciousness" (Kuhlewind 1988).

To further the schooling of consciousness that works congruently with the spiritual mission of Michael, which "enkindles enthusiasm in the feelings, so that the human mind can be filled with devotion for all that can be experienced in the *light of thought*" (Steiner 1973a, 53), psychotherapists can offer guided visualizations, exercises in attention, and instruction in meditation. Beyond these preparatory efforts, which purify and enhance our creative forces and often stimulate the success-ful breaking of previously intractable and self-destructive habits, the work of psychotherapy is to separate our cognitive processes from their entrapment in the world-picture of materialism so that we can begin to practice the observation of our own thinking. Entering into this practice, where we observe our thoughts through sense-free or meditative think-ing (Steiner 1995a; Kühlewind 1988), method and content become one and the same. During this extraordinary state of spiritual consciousness, wherein the practitioner is independent of the spatiality of the physical body, all contrasts, such as ego and world, subject and object, concept and percept, collapse into unity. This thinking, which produces and explains itself without reference to an external object, testifies to the fact that truth can arise only through the human being and as a free creation of the human spirit. Moreover, it is only from this experience of *freedom* that there emerges the capacity for *living thinking* whereby we are able to consciously generate life-filled imaginative pictures that portray the reality of the spiritual worlds.

Affirming the spiritual dimension within, behind, and beyond the apparent physical world, living thinking is animate with a vitality that leads us to an appreciation of our etheric body and the etheric life forces. From Steiner's spiritual-scientific investigations, we have a description of the etheric body as comprised of formative life forces whose "streaming movements" are engaged in the processes of growth and nourishment that maintain the physical body's structure and organization. In addition, it is the human etheric body and its microcosmic world of flowing, weaving thought-images that contains our intellect. According to Steiner's researches, it would be an error to believe that all our thoughts are self-generated, or to presuppose that our thoughts originate in the biochemistry of the brain. Rather, given Steiner's observation that the same cosmic forces that shape and permeate the physical body serve as the medium for our thinking, and that our affective-cognitive life participates in the thought-filled life of the cosmos, it is important for our well-being that we allow ourselves to imaginatively open to the fact that our thinking is permeated by the activity and intentionality of spiritual beings.

Because both thinking and health are activities of the etheric domain, and because the human etheric body can and does receive supersensible impressions from the spiritual worlds, living thinking and therapeutic healing are inherently connected. From this awareness, it is clear that the cultivation of the metamorphosis of ordinary linear thinking into living thinking is a priority of a psychotherapy that would be a schooling of consciousness, a true "*logos* of the soul." Doubtless, working along the disciplined path offered by Steiner facilitates the realization of this goal, which also recognizes and affirms that "The Age of Michael has dawned. Hearts are beginning to have thoughts; spiritual fervour is now proceeding, not merely from mystical obscurity, but from souls clarified by thought" (1973a, 53–54). Consequently, once the work of psychotherapy is committed to uncovering the intimate connections between our own spirituality and the spirituality of the world, as well as to promoting the optimal affective-cognitive conditions for learning living thinking, we can receive Michael into our hearts and begin to neutralize the dehumanizing effects of Lucifer and Ahriman.

Conclusion

The vocation of psychotherapy finds itself in a world besieged by various and insidious forms of violence that increasingly threaten not only the physical and emotional health of the individual but also the survival of the earth. As a consequence of this fact, the practice of psychotherapy, regardless of the presenting problem of the patient or the theoretic orientation of the therapist, occurs as an encounter between people concerned with healing and knowledge that is grounded in a search for meaning. For the practitioner of psychotherapy, the constant of this encounter is that another person comes toward us and calls us to attention. Embedded within the condition of suffering as the place where questioning arises, this call to attention, which is also a call to *give* attention, is always the approach of a mystery. Accepting that the practice of psychotherapy is an encounter with the mystery of the other, which renders any preoccupation with symptom resolution superficial, if not contradictory and possibly destructive, the psychotherapist renounces both the role of problem solver and the goal of psychic repair. Instead, the psychotherapist allows this encounter with and into the mystery of the other, constituted as a journey whose destination is both the unknown interior and the interior of the unknown, to be guided by an openhearted presence that is permeated by wonder, compassion, and hope. Furthermore, as the psychotherapist recognizes that the mystery of the other can only be fathomed by acknowledging the other's spiritual essence, a form of perceiving emerges that is animated by empathic attunement, listening deeply in silence and creative imagination. Unfolding as an openhearted presence where perceiving proceeds alongside the disappearance of preconceptions, the psychotherapeutic encounter can begin the schooling of consciousness necessary for the development of the new affective-cognitive capacity of living thinking.

For the therapist, beyond getting to know the other outwardly and gaining deeper insights into his or her history and future possibilities, the question always remains: what does this particular encounter with this singular other human being truly ask of me? Firstly, it asks that I hear in the other's speaking and silence a vulnerability that not only commands my surrender but also demands, beyond my own interests and at the cost of my own autonomy, my responsibility. Additionally, it asks that I be aware that any communication I offer is, at best, self-explanatory. For the other, I must be as conscious as possible that my communication is perhaps enigmatic and seductive, and that transference, the ubiquitous movement of affectivity and identification that cuts across the frames of time and is always already present, cannot be avoided. Its fruitless repetition, however, can be creatively countered if inspired ways of feeling and living are attentively and patiently nurtured in the here-and-now of our therapeutic relationship. And, however else we may answer the question, this encounter asks that I recognize the other's freedom of thought; for tolerance for the other's thinking is the bedrock of ethical responsibility upon which successful individuation and social transformation depends.

Beyond these relative absolutes faced by the therapist, all of which facilitate psychotherapeutic healing and further the commitment to confronting the terrors that rupture human relationships, there remains the lingering question: what does the event of encounter want, not only of its participants, but for itself? The human encounter, and especially the psychotherapeutic encounter, beckons us to approach and appreciate each other as emanations of the divine, "made in the image and likeness of God." Failing to sense, perceive, and read this ever-present but frequently occluded sign, which can always come into manifestation when two or more beings come together in a human encounter, psychology will remain a soulless science and psychotherapy will shrink from the task of caring for and manifesting the sacred. On the other hand, when psychotherapy helps diminish the terror of this epoch, where pathology increasingly shows itself to be operating under the sign of evil, its practice of encounter finds ways to foster an initiatic consciousness that motivates "every person to become an awakening being to everyone he meets" (Steiner 1974, 155).

Affirming and understanding the urgency of awakening to our spiritual aspect enables the psychotherapeutic encounter to prepare us to receive Michael into our hearts. Countering the terror that presents itself in all sorts of religious doctrine and ritual garb yet transgresses every form of holiness, anthroposophic psychotherapy serves the creative and peaceful impulse of Michael by offering protection and shelter to the mystery of the Other. Aware that as long as human beings are stuck in some state of imbalance between Luciferic and Ahrimanic forces we are prevented from any authentic appreciation of the sacred or participation in the unfolding of Christ consciousness, anthroposophic psychotherapy aims to dissolve our egoistic attachments, even and especially to spirituality, as well as to build up, in an embodied form, the quality of selflessness that is capable of forgiveness, sacrifice, and reverence.

Moreover, by developing our capacity for living thinking as a form of perception that ethically resists both the methodical planning and the unintended thoughtlessness that characterize the disaster that is terror, anthroposophic psychotherapy advocates the improvised play of freely formed thoughts as the optimal way to revitalize interpersonal relationships and social institutions. Additionally, by affirming and encouraging living thinking, anthroposophic psychotherapy facilitates attaining the "etheric clairvoyance" that is necessary for rendering visible the world of the spirit. As an inherently creative stage in the evolution of consciousness, the spirit vision made possible by modern "etheric clairvoyance" is the affective-cognitive precondition for the revelations of an unknown destiny that can *diffuse* the catastrophically fused relations between terror and evil, *infuse* this new space of openness with healing forces permeated by post-Golgothan, "en-Christened" love.

Chapter 6

INTUITIVE AND INCEPTUAL THINKING:
THE MEDITATIVE PATHS OF STEINER
AND HEIDEGGER

I IN ORDER TO understand the conditions favorable for the attainment of a modern initiatic consciousness, we shall focus on the ways that Rudolf Steiner and Martin Heidegger each concerned themselves with the chaotic and potentially creative conditions that characterize our time. We will be guided by the two following imaginations. Steiner claims that at the end of the twentieth century "humanity will either stand at the grave of all civilization—or at the beginning of that Age when in their hearts men ally Intelligence with Spirituality" (1971, 163). Alongside this prophetic statement, we will also take into account Martin Heidegger's claim that "To healing Being first grants ascent into grace; to raging its compulsion to malignancy" (1962b, 238). From both of these pronouncements, the attainment of a modern initiatic consciousness compels us to consider the relationship between human beings and the world, not simply from the point of view of politics and ethics, but especially spiritually and philosophically.

While the attainment of a modern initiatic consciousness requires a change in the structure of political and social relations that demonstrates a commitment to economic redistribution of wealth, civil justice, a sustainable ecology, and the establishment of physical and mental health (to name just a few issues), it necessitates more than positing new contents, however ethical. Consequently, our present challenges cannot be resolved by either rehabilitating traditional modes of thought or by importing the spiritual practices of the past. Rather, in the struggle with the complex reality of terror, which intrudes upon our everyday manner of taking things for granted and estranges us from the commonality of things in ways that render us uncertain if not disconsolate, it is "thinking" itself, the essence of what it means to be human, that must be transformed. In so far as the underlying web of affiliations that constitutes reality is exposed to relentless and diverse forms of terror, it is terror itself that inspires human thinking to become spiritual-philosophical.

Guided by the discourses of Steiner and Heidegger, we will attempt to identify new ways of thinking that can open toward the attainment of modern initiatic consciousness. While Steiner seeks to understand the evolution of human consciousness as a process of cosmic evolution, Heidegger's abiding concern is the "question of Being." Yet both approach the modern relationship between human beings and the world animated by an awareness that egoism and technology have become the dominant forces in our lives, thereby closing off pathways that would affirm spiritual realities or even inaugurate a questioning that meditates upon the essence of truth. Moreover, both Steiner and Heidegger recognize that egoism and technology emerge from the historical occurrence whereby subjectivity, with its positing of the autonomy of the ego, has become the defining principle of what it means to be human. Relying almost exclusively upon the powers of rationality to assert, console, and consolidate itself, the modern subject encounters the world of nature and others as objects. From this disposition, whose essential procedure is quantification and standardization, and whose justification is stability and continuity, the modern subject employs technical devices to reduce nature to calculable stockpiles of available energy while regarding other beings as merely disposable pawns in the game of "me-first" self-aggrandizement and self-preservation.

Given the highly organized operational machinations and violent thoughtlessness that characterize the devastation of the world under the contemporary reign of terror, both Steiner and Heidegger, each in his own style, elucidate forms of a transitive thinking which rejects and departs from the demand for a system. Embarking from Heidegger's provocation that what is "most thought-provoking in our thought-provoking time is that we are still not thinking" (1968, 6), let us see how their explorations of meditative and imaginal living thinking contribute to the transformative crossings necessary for our attainment of modern initiatic consciousness.

Steiner

While by its comprehensive nature and sheer volume Steiner's teaching of the "new mysteries" (Prokofieff 1994) defies any singular definition, the movement he founded, Anthroposophy, can be understood as a "wisdom path." Put into a historical framework beginning with the civilizational demise caused by the drowning of Atlantis, Steiner, especially in *Esoteric Science* (1997a), describes the evolution of cultural epochs. Not content to attribute the development of wisdom to changes in theoretical "worldviews," Steiner is keenly aware that historical transformation results from radical rearrangements in the relationship between human beings and the world, i.e., consciousness. For example, during the first post-Atlantean (Ancient Indian) Epoch, human beings, nostalgic for their spiritual home, tended to regard the world as Maya, the place of illusions. Yet in the second (Ancient Persian) Epoch, influenced by the teachings of Zarathustra, human beings began to regard the world as a place of action, where they could take part in the conflict between the divinities of light and the divinities of darkness, and undertook the beginnings of agriculture. By the fourth (Greco-Roman) Epoch, human beings achieved a balance between the spiritual and physical worlds whereby the gods became incorporated into civil life and served as the original inspiration for poetry, politics, and education. Yet the delicate union between human beings and the world, inspired by the sense of wonder that found expression in the thinking of Sophocles, Pythagoras, Anaximander, Parmenides, and Heraclitus, was not to last. Starting with the Platonic Doctrine of Eternal Forms, the unity between nature and spirit dissolved and the world was divided into sensible things and supersensible ideas. As a consequence of this bifurcation, these domains began to stand opposed to each other, and there arose the dualism between Being and beings. This dualism then served as the foundation for the decline of wisdom-based philosophy into logic-based metaphysical thinking.

A more radical transition took place in the relationship between human beings and the world at the beginning of the fifth (Modern) Epoch. In this epoch, which commenced in the middle of the fifteenth century, human beings began to experience the world as exclusively physical, and the notion of God began to lose meaning. Absolutely closed off from the spiritual realm, human beings now encountered the world mainly through the forming of hypotheses about nature. With this development, the essence of nature was experienced only in concepts designed to determine its usefulness for satisfying human goals. Alongside the disenchantment of nature, the development of materio-metaphysical thinking shaped a new and very specific understanding of human beings. Positing the idea of a rational animal, materio-metaphysical thinking implies that human beings consist of an instinctive structure derived from their animal heritage as well as a capacity for reason that is a vestige of their spiritual ancestry. From this idea of the rational animal, we can see that materio-metaphysical thinking adapts a zoological definition to ground the previously established dualism between nature and spirit, and implants it directly into its understanding of the human being.

The remnants of interconnectedness between human beings and the world began to disappear with the arising of the identity postulated by Descartes between thinking and existence. To secure this identity, which requires that human beings and the world exist independently of each other, thinking is associated with the capacity for reason, and this capacity for "clear and distinct ideas" is understood to be the privilege of the human being. Under the imperatives of materio-metaphysical thinking, human existence is validated by reason; hence the human being becomes a subject whose subjectivity is predicated upon its ability to render itself objective. After establishing its own subjectivity through self-alienation, the human being validates itself by subjugating the world to its reason. With the triumph of Cartesian materio-metaphysical thinking, human beings, through their identification with an objectifying reason, render their relationship with the world problematic. Isolated from all other beings, human beings take on the role of dominating the world as a matter of right.

The materio-metaphysical thinking that grants human beings seemingly unrestrained mastery over other beings and things has persisted as the dominant worldview during the modern epoch. Yet it would obviously be an egregious mistake to see the expansion of reason, which follows from the contraction of divine or indeed any other influence on the immediate sphere of human experience, as a wholly negative happening. Rather, as Steiner repeatedly points out, as human beings are left to relate to the world without spiritual guidance, we find ourselves called upon to permeate our actions with freedom. Alongside our newly gained freedom, the expansion of reason supports the enhancement of individuality, greater economic productivity, and the maturity of conscience. Yet while these secularizing processes define the uniqueness of the modern epoch, which Steiner associates with the advent of the consciousness soul, their positive unfolding is neither a given nor is it free of side effects. Specifically, there is the danger that freedom will degenerate into the abuse of power, and that individuality will collapse into narcissism and egoism. Certainly the augmentation of rational control over the outer world through technological virtuosity, and the inability to free the inner world from instinctive compulsion, has become the normative reality of the modern epoch. Constrained by the historical evolution of materio-metaphysical thinking, the modern relationship between human beings and the world increasingly results in conflicts between oppositional and absolutist claims or needs whose dangerous polarizations defy, if not preclude, resolution.

As a response to modern materio-metaphysical epistemology, which fails to attribute consciousness to the external world, Steiner embarked upon the redemption of thinking necessary to the evolutionary progress of freedom. Addressing this need in the book he felt would have the most enduring effect of all his writings, *Intuitive Thinking as a Spiritual Path*, Steiner offered a theory of knowledge that seeks to overcome the tendency to "direct our attention only to the object of our thinking, and not simultaneously to our thinking itself" (1995a, 79). To overcome this tendency, which is endemic to the present human organization, we must first recognize that thinking is the activity that most definitively characterizes us as a species. Yet it is crucial that this recognition not lead us to accept the naïve belief that thinking is primarily personal or is to be understood by reference to subjective feelings or sensation. Rather, thinking is prior to the thoughts of a subject; the concepts we form take shape in wordless thinking. That is, thinking, which is universal, precedes even the relation that separates a subject from an object. As Steiner writes,

> It is not the subject that introduces the relationship, but think-ing. The subject does not think because it is a subject; rather, it appears to itself as a subject because it can think.... I should never say that my individual subject thinks; rather, it lives by the grace of thinking. Thus, thinking is an element which leads me beyond myself and unites me with objects. But it separates me from them at the same time, by setting me over against them as subject." (Ibid., 52–53)

Through the grace of thinking, human beings are able to formulate concepts and achieve a separate existence from objects. At the same time, through the grace of thinking human beings are able to achieve self-transcendence and independent relationships. For Steiner, it is the grace of thinking "that establishes the double nature of the human being": simultaneously an individual and at one with the world (Ibid.).

While human beings are indebted to the grace of thinking for their individuality, an element other than thinking is also required. This element is perception. As the element through which human beings observe the world outside of any conscious activity, perception reveals the aggregate of *sensory reality*. This aggregate can be called the object of observation—objects that human beings come to know by creating *percepts* (Ibid., 54). In contrast to the uniformity of concepts, percepts are always personal and, as such, highly significant. From the totality of experience, percepts are what singularizes or individuates one's thinking and subjectivity.

It must be noted that the self is also a percept. Enclosing the self or "I" within the realm of personality, self-perception veils the multi-dimensionality of the human being and severs its connection to other possibilities for being. As such, self-perception yields no self-knowledge. Rather, knowledge is the synthesis of the conceptual content with the percept—a synthesis created by the inner activity of thinking. It is intuition, the ever-present origin that sustains the activity of thinking (Ibid., 88). Intuition not only supplies us with the content that is absent from the percept, but also allows thinking to join together everything that we separate in perception. Finally, when the result of the relation between intuition and a specific percept is retained as an "individualized concept," human beings form "mental pictures" (Ibid., 100) that serve as the basis of individual experience.

The quality of our experience, its textures and tones, continues to depend upon our ability to find intuitions that correspond to the percept. Yet, while reality reveals itself to us in concepts and percepts, and mental pictures are the subjective representation of this revelation, the quality of our experience is not reducible only to thinking. We also relate the percept to our subjectivity, to our individual "I." "The expression of this individual relation is feeling, which manifests as pleasure or displeasure" (Ibid., 101). Through feeling, which concretizes the concept with vitality, an individual relates to the world from within the particular intensities of his or her own being. As the expression of the specific dispositions and moods of the personality, feeling complements thinking and promotes the orientation of the dual nature of the human being toward wholeness.

Thus far we have followed Steiner's epistemological investigations as they pertain to the theoretical conditions for the establishment of human freedom. Yet if this epistemology is to contribute to the transformations necessary for the attainment of a modern initiatic consciousness, the process of thinking must become a living experience—that is, our "I"-consciousness must become *present* to its own experience.

Steiner describes this occurrence as requiring an "immersion brought about by a power that flows through the activity of thinking itself—this power is love in its spiritual form" (Ibid., 120). He continues, "Of this spiritual essence we can say that it becomes present to our consciousness through intuition. Intuition is the conscious experience, within what is purely spiritual, of a purely spiritual content" (Ibid., 136–37).

Therefore, if our "I"-consciousness is to grasp the nature of living thinking, that "I"-consciousness must become present for the reception of intuitions. Yet this presence requires that we surrender sense-perception as the vehicle for knowledge, for "the human organization of body and soul can have no effect on the *essence* of thinking" (Ibid.). Unfortunately, the realization that body and soul are impediments to knowledge is impossible as long as ordinary "I"-consciousness remains enthralled by the products of remembered thoughts and saturated by historically-induced feelings. Hence it is only by opening itself up to a new and higher stage of consciousness that our "I"-consciousness can become *present* for the receipt of intuitions.

We do not accomplish this opening via any intellectual endeavor, for this would yield only thinking about thinking. Rather, according to anthroposophist and cognitive scientist Georg Kühlewind, we cultivate receptivity to this spiritual reality by undertaking meditative practices that strengthen "concentrated attention" (1984; 1988). In this way our "I"-consciousness is both more able to come into contact with the living spiritual presence and more open to the experience of intuition; i.e., we become present to the activity of thinking.

When we become present to the flashing up of intuition, our "I"-consciousness is no longer embedded in everyday reality. Rather, with the unmediated illumination of consciousness there emerges, even if only for a moment, our true or originary "I." The emergence of our originary "I," like the essence of living thinking, is a unique event that reveals the unfolding of a purely spiritual content and context. That our "I"-consciousness opens to the singularity of this emergence through the meditative practices of "concentrated attention" attests to the fact that our ordinary thoughts and perceptions are but partial approximations of the truth of being. Consequently, if we are to overcome these falsifications, which are the basis of all our sufferings and inhibit the fulfillment of our freedom, we must enhance our cognitive faculties. Thus, the emergence of our originary "I," which opens us to becoming present for intuitions, turns us inescapably toward thinking through the question that serves as the source for all self-knowledge: who am "I"?

To think through this existential question is to quest for self-transformation; it is to seek the truth of one's selfhood, which is not possible for our ordinary "I"-consciousness. Thinking through this question, I perceive, for example, that "I am" not my body, for the "I am" carries an intuitive knowledge that it is not confined to the body. And as I think through this question, I realize that all of the activities that define my ordinary "I"-consciousness are not-me, for I am the one who determines these definitions. Thinking through this question, I find that every concept, perception, feeling, and object is not-me, for all these thoughts are nonessential to me. Thinking through this question, I realize that I must surrender all that is not-me if I am to arrive at my originary "I." Surrendering all that is not-me, the only answer that thinking can offer to this question is the undeniable reality that the originiary "I" *is*. At its core, shorn of all the attachments that perpetuate self-feeling, my originary "I" is nothing other than that it *is*. My originary "I" is no-thing and it contains no-thing of content other than that it *is*: "I am" that "I am."

Thinking through the question "Who am I?" has allowed us to arrive at an experience of the originary "I." Yet thinking itself has still escaped observation. Thinking through the question has hidden from us that the "I am" is still identified with thinking. Precisely because thinking is so close to our soul, this identification is the most difficult to notice and to overcome. Yet this overcoming is necessary because, as Kühlewind emphasizes, "even thinking is something external for this "I." This "I" is not outside itself: it is an absolute beingness, a primal spirit-being, that draws its meaning out of itself" (1984, 50).

As a "primal spirit-being," the "I am" is our spirit self. Understanding itself as its own source, the "I am" does not need to submerge or ground itself in thinking. Standing under itself and liberated from any identification with thinking, the "I am" can activate its capacity to observe and thereby grasp the essence of thinking. Exercising this capacity, the "I am" "celebrates the *primal deed of spirit*: it cognizes itself and thus creates itself" (Ibid.). When the "I am" engages in this living thinking, which can only originate from the realm of its own cognitive creativity, it gives rise to an inner experience of truth that has nothing to do with correctness, or with measuring a present, living consciousness against some past content of consciousness. Exceeding any doctrine of correspondence or adequacy, the inner experience of truth that resonates to the cognitive creativity of the "I am" is a dynamic event, disclosing and manifesting the substantial essence of life itself. This living substance, the primal substance of the cosmos that permeates the "I am" and suffuses our thinking and feeling, is "love in its spiritual form." In the experience of the "I am," cognition and love flow together as a "single life-stream that gives evidence of the fundamental experience of the spirit" (Ibid.).

More than simply attaining awareness and experience of our originary "I am," modern initiatic consciousness entails bringing that awareness and experience into the relationship between human beings and the world so that this relationship may fulfill Steiner's "fundamental maxim for *free human beings*: To *live* in love of action, and *to let live* in understanding of the other's will" (Ibid., 155). Insofar as we are free only when our actions display the moral consciousness that characterizes the "I am"—a consciousness that retreats from self-hardening and selflessly opens a spiritually informed *love* to the otherness of our neighbors—modern initiatic consciousness displays its authenticity when it facilitates a transformation of our faculty of thinking to the point that it becomes an inner experience of truth that is not only knowledge, but also life, deed, and sentiment.

Intuitive, living thinking permits our "I am" to experience the truth that cognition is being. From the moment this experience of truth springs into the soul, however, its transmutation into love usually takes place in reference to the will to power, whose unifying purpose is to increase the fullness and power of things and to strive to overcome new obstacles. Severing the creative and nurturing interplay between the inner experience of truth and the "I am," the nihilistic application of the will to power inflicts the violence of irrelevance upon the continuity of living cosmic intelligence and romanticizes, if not diminishes, the spiritual source of love. Countering this devastation of the relationship between humans and the world, intuitive thinking frees the seeker of wisdom and truth, who in this epoch of terror can only be each and every one of us, from enslavement to the apparently real "outer" world, and guides us into the "inner" world of cognition. In this turning of perception, our attention is liberated from its obsessions with the surface appearances of beings and things, and in this clearing there ensues an openness where "love is freely expressed for the contents of a world that does not yet exist, so that it can become" (Kühlewind 1987, 49).

While modern initiatic consciousness promotes this futural turning, intuitive thinking facilitates the maturation of the soul. As the cognitive process that enhances the integration of such qualities as self-confidence, humility, self-control, gentleness, presence of mind, and steadfastness (Steiner 1995c, 22), intuitive thinking encourages a morality consistent with preserving rather than challenging the essence of a being or thing. As the cognitive core of the spiritual path that both serves the selfless-ness of the "consciousness soul" and conserves the indestructible origin that is the "I am," intuitive thinking is identical with "heart thinking" (Steiner 1995a; Kühlewind 1987). Immersing itself within the essence of truth, heart thinking exemplifies the soul-spiritual reality that we experi-ence in meditation, wherein the inner movement of thinking a theme allows us to become one with the theme. When engaging in a "thinking of the heart," not only are we "within the Beings and things themselves" (Steiner 1995a, 165), but we are also engaged in a living practice that is devoted to ensouling the world. As an antidote to the deadening of vital-ity that emerges into the world from materio-metaphysical constructions of reality, whose loyalty to technoscience always privileges divisiveness over union and control over truth, "thinking of the heart" offers the relationship between human beings and the world a healthy hopefulness composed of spiritual wisdom and love.

Heidegger

To introduce the philosophical thinking of Martin Heidegger, which is never a comprehensive system but is always a dynamic path of question-ing Being that is on the way toward transformative possibilities, let us attend to the speech he gave as a "Memorial Address" to celebrate the 175th birthday of the composer Conradin Kreutzer. This lecture, usually referred to as "Gelassenheit," (DT) is superficially a comparison between two modes of thought: calculative and meditative thinking. But this surface offering conceals a deeper and more abiding concern: that an ever-growing obsession with technology, which shapes the contours of our practical life with its proliferation of enjoyable, often necessary, and sometimes redundant products, also obscures and forecloses divergent forms of relating to beings, thereby limiting or eliminating other ways of participating in the world.

At work whenever we "plan, research and organize" (46), calculative thinking is characterized by subordinating given conditions to very specific purposes so that they yield the definite results that we want. Functioning according to a means-ends rationality and a mode of investigation that relies upon the measures and standards provided by statistical probability, calculative thinking gives us something we can count on. Providing us with the certainty that allows for speedy and efficient problem-solving and with a method that promotes the achievement of goals, calculative thinking facilitates the productivity necessary for "business as usual." Within this increasingly specialized and dense network structure, which is thoroughly utilitarian and therefore refrains from deliberating upon the meaning that inheres in every being and thing, especially the natural world, calculative thinking is highly operational. Yet herein lies its danger.

Precisely because the utilitarian orientation toward beings and things is so successful at extracting the energies necessary for running modern economies, calculative thinking captivates our attention and structures our life-world. Distracted by gadgets, information, and strategic programs that, while apparently designed to help us to become more "ourselves," actually aid in concealing our dangerous self-obsession, we fail to recognize that the technological pursuit of progress rests upon the assumption that the world is simply made up of resources for us to exploit. As calculative thinking establishes its normative principles over all areas of life, there arises what Heidegger calls the loss of "rootedness and autochthony" (Ibid., 48–49). Functioning behind a seemingly endless supply of instantly replaceable commodities, calculative thinking, in its relentless attack upon the beings and things of the world, promotes the "*flight from thinking* that is the ground of thoughtlessness" (Ibid., 45).

Note, however, that Heidegger does not present the accelerated imposition of challenging and entertaining technologies as the true danger that threatens contemporary existence. According to Heidegger, that danger lies in the possibility that human beings will become so enchanted by the conveniences produced by calculative thinking that we will forget to dwell within the thinking that is most genuine and proper to us, the thinking that is most essentially ours as human beings: that is, *meditative thinking*.

Heidegger stresses that meditative thinking is nothing "high-flown" (Ibid., 47). Not restricted to specialists or spiritualists, meditative thinking can occur on any occasion and wherever we find ourselves, if only we attend to what concerns us most intimately. Meditative thinking ponders the beings and things that compose the intimacies of our world for the sake of disclosing that which makes them what they are. Meditative thinking also contemplates what is even closer to us—Being itself—for it is only in the light of Being, as that which is closest and originary (though withdrawn from our ordinary perception), that we can come to an understanding of what it means *to be* in general and how to relate to the beings and things of the world. Indeed, it is only in the light of Being that the dynamic *arising and unfolding* of those things and beings, rather than their apparently durable presence, can be disclosed to meditative thinking in ways that are neither fascinating, insistent, nor enslaving.

Heidegger's plea that we engage in meditative thinking is not offered in of opposition to technology. Rather, it reflects his awareness that technology makes a claim on us, the exclusivity of which precludes all other claims. Yet he declares that meditative thinking can allow us to see through the seeming imperviousness of calculative thinking and technology, and to gain independence from their thrall. As an invocation of a more essential dimension that regulates the relationship between the world and human beings, the meditative thinking that contemplates Being deposes calculative thinking from its sovereign role as meaning giver and neutralizes the exclusive power of technological things. Consequently, Heidegger's question concerning technology is not so much a protest against technology as a plea that we learn to use these things in a detached manner that protects us from becoming victimized.

Let us look directly at Heidegger's disposition toward calculative thinking and technology as well as the hints he offers about how meditative thinking can transform the relationship between the world and ourselves.

We can use technical devices, and yet with proper use also keep ourselves so free of them, that we may let go of them at any time. We can use technical devices as they ought to be used, and also let them alone as something which does not affect our inner and real core. We can affirm the unavoidable use of technical devices, also deny them the right to dominate us, and so to warp, confuse, and lay waste our nature.

But will not saying both yes and no this way to technical devices make our relation to technology ambivalent and insecure? On the contrary! Our relation to technology will become wonderfully simple and relaxed. We let technical devices enter our daily life, and at the same time leave them outside, that is, let them alone, as things which are nothing absolute but remain dependent upon something higher. I would call this comportment toward technology which expresses "yes" and at the same time "no," by an old word, *releasement toward things*.

Having this comportment we no longer view things only in a technical way....There is then in all technical processes a meaning, not invented or made by us, which lays claim to what man does and leaves undone....*The meaning pervading technology hides itself*. But if we explicitly and continuously heed the fact that such hidden meaning touches us everywhere in the world of technology, we stand at once within the realm of that which hides itself from us, and hides itself just in approaching us. That which shows itself and at the same time withdraws is the essential trait of what we call the mystery. I call the comportment which enables us to keep open the meaning hidden in technology, *openness to the mystery* (Ibid., 54–55).

In Heidegger's *releasement toward things*, an attitude of "letting be" prevails that allows us to use technical devices, and yet be free of their negative influence. We can say "yes" to the utilization of technical devices and refuse to be encroached upon by their hypnotic effect. We can refuse to let them take us under their exclusive domination. We can say "yes" and "no" at the same time to their priorities. By simply letting technical devices be—i.e., letting them do what they were made to do—we can inaugurate a simple and peaceable relationship to things. *Releasement* expresses this mode of detachment.

At the same time as we practice attaining *releasement toward things*, Heidegger asks us to notice that technical devices "remain dependent upon something higher." What is the "higher" realm, the "higher" claim that we adhere to when we engage in meditative thinking? Given the omnipresence of technical devices, what is it that "hides itself just in approaching us"? What is it that offers itself while withdrawing from us? What is it that is most obvious and yet most easily falls into oblivion? To these enigmatic questions, Heidegger answers: Being. Being is the mystery. Consequently, the meditative thinking that contemplates Being, turning away from the bondage that results from the thoughtless idealization and idolatry of technology, is inseparable from *openness to the mystery*.

While these comportments belong together, they cannot be said to "belong" to humans as techniques that can be mastered or appropriated. Rather than programs for self-improvement, strategies for a sustainable environment, or procedures for experiencing spiritual enlightenment, releasement toward things and openness to the mystery are "grants and promises" that announce the possibility of transforming our relations to the groundless ground of being and which establish how we dwell in the world. Releasement can "give us a vision of a new autochthony" (Ibid.) and grant us the conditions conducive for healing the "rootlessness" that results from the dominance of calculative thinking. Yet, Heidegger maintains that human beings will fail to bring clarity to this vision of realizing a genuine homeland if we remain attached to finding its ground in subjectivity. Rather, does not the displacement that defines the "spirit" of the age of global reach require a meditative thoughtfulness that envisions the entire cosmos as our homeland and makes us cosmic beings?

Even if we attain the capacity to dwell in the freedom to say "yes" and "no" to technology, mere human beingness cannot be the ground of this new rootedness. If we are to our rootedness, in releasement, we must turn away from any form of humanism that supports the illusion that our calculations and needs provide the rationales for our future world. In this deepening of meditative thinking, releasement is the condition upon which mystery can manifest itself. And insofar as the mystery is Being, releasement allows Being to unfold in a way that lets human beings open to the unknown without fear. Releasement designates that human thinking and Being's openness are identical, for releasement is what both Being and thinking, or human being, does. As it relates to the founding of a new homeland and the creating of new forms of self-other-world awareness, releasement lets Being come into presence as the transition toward human beings. Only in this transition, which takes place in openness to the mystery, can Being release itself and grant human beings their dwelling. At the same time, it is only in this transition that human beings can realize freedom in a way that lets us truly receive the gift of Being and become engaged on a path that leads to new grounds for dwelling in the world.

While the reciprocity between releasement and openness to the mystery prepares us for the new autochthony, this occurrence "does not befall us accidentally" (Ibid., 56). What is required for this new dwelling-site is the persistence of meditative thinking as a "courageous thinking" (Ibid.). Meditative thinking is courageous when it furthers letting human beings pursue living in the mystery of being. This persistence, which only arises in our detachment from the "raging" desire to be the cause of transformation, shows itself as the capacity for an active receiving that can await the bestowal of Being. At the same time, meditative thinking that persists in the mystery of being is courageous when it envelops the totality of beings present in the human heart. This courage, which arises when we detach ourselves from the belief that information derived from the sense-perception of objects constitutes knowledge, shows the human heart to be the center of the thinking that maintains an open and innocent relation with the mystery.

Releasement lets the beings and things of the world disclose themselves as belonging together in the light of Being. As releasement, Being gives itself to thinking. Its gift, which is the possibility of a rooted dwelling that speaks from the essence of the mystery of Being to the mystery of the essence of human being, requires that we completely reverse our habitual ways of being in the world; instead of adhering to the indifferent thoughtlessness of calculating principles, we must begin to think with an open heart. For it is only in thinking with an open heart, which is to truly engage the path of meditative thinking, that we will arrive at that "ground of creativity which produces lasting works" (Ibid., 57).

Conclusion

While obvious differences exist in the questions and vocabularies that guide the meditative paths of Steiner and Heidegger, both thinkers are particularly attuned to the dangers that egoism and technology pose to the relationship between human beings and the world. Profoundly concerned that these manifestations of the materio-metaphysical worldview constrict our possibilities for freedom, Steiner elaborates an epistemology that demonstrates not only how the thoughts of our ordinary "I"-consciousness conceal ethical intuitions, but also how these intuitions, when liberated from body-and-brain-based sensing, can enliven our thinking, feeling, and willing to the point where the spiritual world can enter into relationship with us and guide our deeds. For Steiner, intuitive thinking is the precondition for the attaining of cognitive capacities that allow the human being to "sense the inner schism between his dwarf-like existence on earth and the experience that lights up within him of himself as a cosmic being" (1988, 116).

Heidegger, on the other hand, is called to meditative thinking in response to the way technology contributes to the oblivion of Being. Observing that technological systems of production and circulation, in ordering and delivering the resources necessary for perpetuating the business of everyday life, reduce all beings, including human beings, to raw material, Heidegger emphasizes that our sense of security consists in nothing more than the idolatry of technology. As the material successes of calculative thinking become increasingly spectacular and the availability of replaceable technical devices becomes virtually limitless, Heidegger enjoins us to contemplate how the resourcefulness of technology gives rise to an estrangement from Being that promotes ecological destruction, psychological emptiness, and social alienation. Moreover, as technology replaces the unique with the exchangeable, and value with exchange value, the reality of the world as a place for the display of difference and the play of opposites that characterizes creativity and art collapses. In fostering this disappearance of distinction, which coincides with the "frantic abolition of all distances [that] brings no nearness" (PLT, 165), technology is linked by Heidegger to the contemporary historical manifestation that we know as the universalization of terror.

The dangers and distresses egoism and technology inflict upon the relationship between human beings and the world, as well as upon Being itself, amount to nothing less than radical dehumanization and the repression of any possibility of revelation. As a response to these evils, perhaps the most courageous and resolute task to be undertaken by those aspiring to a modern initiatic consciousness is to intuitively and meditatively think "releasement to the mystery" as a path of letting-be that refuses all forms of fundamentalisms, including humanism and religion, while embracing those singular events of presencing that sanctify the places where heartfelt and sheltering encounters, either between souls or between humans and spiritual beings, are granted possibility.

Chapter 7

"WHILE MY CONSCIENCE EXPLODES"...

THE PERNICIOUSNESS of nihilism at the beginning of twenty-first century would shock even Nietzsche. In addition to the relentless militarism that has come to dominate government policy and human life, nihilism fosters destructive conditions that include but are not limited to the ingestion and injection of ever more chemically refined intoxicants, the unregulated exposure to faster and more detailed technological systems and information networks, widespread political and religious fundamentalisms, and the unceasing demand for natural and synthetic energies. Increasingly constructing our experience of the basic self-other-world relational dynamic within an atmosphere thundering alternately with destabilizing fragmentation and compulsive totalization, nihilism blocks the development of mutual respect necessary for psychosocial health, let alone justice and peace. Beyond the insidious consolations offered by an entertainment industry committed to a version of "reality" based on survival skills, get-rich-quick schemes, the cult of celebrity, and occasional flights of ecstatic fantasy, nihilism enforces the psychosocial law of gravity: deflation, depletion, and deficiency.

As these negative dynamics become psychologically internalized and physically incorporated, the essential human capacity for attention becomes arranged within a phenomenology of dissociation. Impeding the development of focused awareness and fracturing the process of affect regulation into oscillations between compulsive renunciation and

gluttonous consumption, nihilism gives rise to diffused forms of concentration, rigid patterns of organization, hyperactivity, and structural
dysfunction. Encroaching upon the "autonomy of the conscious subject"
(Kühlewind 1983), symptomatic episodes of time-warping, space-jumps,
associative scattering and inexplicable (dis)appearances have emerged
in ways that psychiatry and psychology have seen fit to diagnose as
attention deficit disorder (DSM IV). Inflicting "attacks on linking"(Bion
1970) within communicative encounters, attention deficit disrupts the
rhythm of presence, thereby frustrating the attainment of personal
integrity and interpersonal intimacies. As attention deficit erodes the
possibility of establishing trust, relational dynamics in all areas of life
verge toward hurtful misunderstandings, enervating codependencies,
and punitive abandonments.

Attention deficit serves the brutality of nihilism beyond the production of divisive psychological symptoms. To mention one example,
attention deficit prevents consideration of public policies according to
their long-term consequences. As decisions are undertaken and laws
enacted according to the needs of the immediate—the reactive approach
of "damage control"—it becomes impossible to compose political relationships around multiple discourses. In the absence of an irreducible
respect for singular differences that simultaneously encourages mutual
interests and reciprocal concern, attention deficit prevents the creation
of institutions that advance the establishment of "civil society."

Beyond the subversion of the legitimacy of the political sphere,
the indiscriminate use of increasingly available electronic media both
promotes attention deficit and insinuates that enacting moral conscience is an unnecessary ordeal. As we increasingly take our cues from
nonhuman devices, personal communication, with all its complexities,
becomes a burden we take up with reluctance, hence through sheer lack
of practice we lose touch with the necessity of employing conscience in
our interactions. Concern for the well-being of others and regard for the
sustainability of the earth recede behind the pragmatics of self-preservation, nationalism, and the unbridled accumulation of financial, natural,
and human resources. Yet while the nihilistic indifference to essentially
moral questions pervades all areas of socioeconomic, techno-scientific,

and artistic activity, our epoch is also witnessing an awakening of soul consciousness that is concerned with ethical questions. This new ethical awareness is not limited to social issues or to the paradoxical effects of scientific advances, but also reflects the intuition, emerging from the depths of the soul and from the surrounding cosmos, of an embracing spiritual reality interweaving with the destiny of earth and humanity.

Attending to the birth and growth of this soul consciousness, a spiritual reality means grounding ethical awareness in responsible social initiatives that arise from attention to the forgotten moral values of truth, beauty, and goodness. Beyond actively resisting the uncritical acceptance of materialism and humanistic relativism, we must protect the emerging awareness of spiritual reality from the detours of spontaneous (unsought) or drug-enhanced mystical experience and the revival of archaic forms of seeking the sacred. Toward this task of providing soul consciousness with grounding and protection, we will delve further into the teachings of Rudolf Steiner and Martin Heidegger.

Offering guidance in healing attention disorders and developing affective-cognitive practices that enhance moral conscience, Steiner builds a wisdom-and-love-based path for attaining knowledge of the spiritual world—a path that not only enhances the individuation process but also challenges the alienation from self and others promulgated by nihilism. Meanwhile, Heidegger, especially in *Being and Time*, presents an existential and unintentionally psychological analysis of authenticity and inauthenticity that invokes the call of conscience. In later works, he takes a turn "on the way to language," revealing an understanding of poetics that suggests an alternative to the modern exhaustion of nature and abandonment of Being.

Steiner: The Birth and Development of Conscience

While it is possible to practice Steiner's teachings for attaining initiatic knowledge without accepting his contention that they are the form appropriate to the structure of the modern soul, it is impossible to realize their intention without coming to terms with his understanding of the evolution of consciousness (1997a). This process requires a momentary retreat from the contemporary situation to a vision of history that Steiner terms *occult*. Always placing his teachings within a socio-cultural process that emphasizes the importance of the ancient event known as the Atlantean Flood, Steiner views this catastrophe as necessitating a migration eastward of small numbers of human beings whose maturation of consciousness prepared them both to survive and to revive humanity. Beginning a post-Atlantean cycle of seven Wisdom Epochs, of which we are now in the fifth (1423–3583), Steiner supports his civilizational perspective with the awareness that the evolution of consciousness is accompanied by a change in human embodiment and cognition. As human beings become more separated from a unity with the beings and forces of the cosmos and more acclimated to the mineral structure of the earth, embodiment and cognition undergo a corresponding process of physicalization.

A major consequence of this dual relocation, from cosmic life to earth life and from world being to body being, is a transformation in the attainment of knowledge. Steiner tells us that the Mysteries of ancient times enshrined a knowledge of the supersensible that was born in the soul and bound up with the element of the moral will. To avoid misuse of this knowledge, which constituted a power in itself, the initiated inducted others into the reality of supersensible knowledge only when the new initiates had undertaken special preparations that enhanced their sense of responsibility toward their people or their race. Consisting of a direct perception of the inner connection between the separate kingdoms of nature, the different members and functions of the human being, and the ordering of the Divine Hierarchies, initiation into the Mysteries always carried an intense moral imperative. With the progress of human evolution, however, came the disappearance of humans' atavistic capacity to see and hear, however dim and dreamlike their perception, the immediate moral effects of their deeds in the spirit world. As a consequence, by the middle of the Greco-Roman Epoch, perception of the moral connection between power and knowledge had all but vanished.

Steiner writes that moral clairvoyant knowledge, which previously connected humanity to the Cosmic Mysteries, had so receded by the time of Aeschylus that only the voices of the Furies were now audible—

and then barely comprehensible. Even Socrates, whose profound philosophical teachings contain remnants of the ancient wisdom, only speaks of the mystery of the "Daimon-Life," his awareness of the "immortality of the Soul," when death has become imminent (Krell 1992). Recognizing that the positive development of humanism and rationalism during the Ancient Greek Epoch corresponds to the loss of a continuous relationship between the human soul and the spiritual world, Steiner maintains that the withering of natural clairvoyant capacities does not eliminate the soul's need to find a moral measure of its deeds. In fact, achievements in the art, literature, philosophy, and politics of the Ancient Greek Epoch reveal the development of a new cognitive capacity that offers a potentially equivalent moral force to compensate for the demise of the old relationship to the gods. Proclaiming this metamorphosis in the human soul as the *birth* of conscience, Steiner writes:

> ...whatever conscience may be, it is experienced as a voice in the individual's breast which determines with irresistible power what is good and what is bad; what a man must do in order to gain his own approval and what he must leave undone in order not to despise himself. Hence we can say: Conscience appears to every individual as something holy in the human breast. (1983b, 102)

According to Steiner, the experience and appearance of conscience is immanent—it happens "in the human breast"—and inseparable from "something holy." The word "holy" tells us that the soul engaged in the evaluative struggle between acceptance and loathing is moved by an engagement with a witnessing function whose role is inherently moral. From this moral perspective, conscience is an experience less concerned with giving specific instructions than with indicating, as Plato proclaims: "the sovereign to whom we must submit if we are ever to become men of worth" (1973a, Laws, III.699). For Steiner, the sovereignty of conscience belongs to the fact that while the "holy" signifies an eternal element in the soul, this eternity is revealed in the dignity of inward judgment that incarnates in time.

Steiner approaches conscience as that which gives voice to the Holy. Yet his sense of the Holy is distinct from Otto's concern with the non-rational elements of the numinous (1976) and from Eliade's differentiation between the sacred and profane (1959). Rather, Steiner is concerned with disclosing how matters of conscience give expression to matters of the heart and soul. Thus, he defines the very *matter* of the soul, or one might say the *heart* of the soul, as "a modification, one of the infinite variety of transformations possible, of that which we call love, provided that we genuinely grasp the intrinsic meaning of this word....love [is] the soul constituent of earthly being" (1995b, 189). Steiner's declaration that love is the essence of soul confirms what we know from everyday experience, that love is the most extraordinary of ordinary human feelings. But, perhaps the spiritual teacher is referring not to ordinary human feeling but to some rare and disembodied love? On the contrary, "Love mediated by way of the senses is the wellspring of creative power, of that which is coming into being. Without senseborn love, nothing created by humanity in the material world would exist" (1998, 182). Regardless of how consonant Steiner's considerations are with our common sense, his understanding of love comes with a proviso: for love to be genuine, given that this feeling is infinitely transformable, its intrinsic meaning, its "fundamental substance," must be comprehensively grasped. Apparently the inherently creative, senseborn feeling of love is not the only or sufficient constituent of genuine love. Consequently, we must assume that there is something in the way we feel love that eludes comprehension of its intrinsic meaning and also deludes the soul.

In order to ascertain what a comprehensive grasp of love entails, let us dwell upon a description offered by Steiner that concerns a dynamic often at work in relations of love.

> A person supposes that he loves another, but in this love really is loving himself....What he feels as a state of rapture in his own soul in association with the other person, what he experiences within himself by reason of the fact that he is in the presence of the other person, that he makes declarations of love, if you please, to the other person—that is what he really loves. In the

whole thing the person loves himself as he kindles this self-love in his social relationship with the other person.

This is an important mystery in human life and it is of enormous importance. This love that a person supposes is real, but that is really only self-love, self-seeking, egoism, masked egoism—is the source of the greatest imaginable and the most widespread antisocial impulses. Through this self-love masked as real love, a person becomes in preeminent degree an antisocial being. (1941, 135–36)

As we regard this description, it becomes clear that a grasp of the inherent meaning of love must include comprehension of the duplicity engendered by the power of egoism. A well-known explanation of this inversion of love, whereby self-love is substituted for love of the other, is given in the psychoanalytic understanding of the mythological figure of Narcissus. Focusing upon Narcissus' infatuation with the mirror image of his own form, psychoanalysis interprets this primal scene of distorted self-observation as a defense against the fear of death and the loss of the love object. Indicative of an inhibited capacity to love, as well as an intolerance of the presence of the other and the reality of the world, narcissism is a form of psychological pathology that manifests vanity, pride, self-absorption, turning away from interpersonal intimacy, and a denial of death. When egoism encapsulates in self-interest rather than becoming permeated by the hope-filled and selfless forces of the ego, which reflects the closing off of awareness to the divine ground of being, real human interconnectedness, heart-felt being with others, evaporates. From this failure of maturation, which is obviously psychological, but more importantly spiritual, comes both the constriction of moral conscience that would express care for the world and others, and the inability to realize the evolutionary impulse for freedom that is identical to universal love. Hence for Steiner, who believed that evil has not existed from the beginning of time but arises from the misuse of inherently good qualities, "the common trait of all evil is nothing other than egoism" (1997b, 25).

To amplify the collusive relationship that Steiner establishes between egoism and evil, as well as to perceive the spiritual background

that structures and perpetuates the soul's difficulties in realizing freedom and attaining universal love, we will return to the workings of
the two spirit-beings that he describes as Lucifer and Ahriman (1993).
Impressing upon us that Lucifer and Ahriman have legitimate tasks
within the cosmic order, including contributing to the formation of the
physical human being out of the "Phantom," or archetypal spirit body
(1973a), as well as to the differentiation between male and female,
Steiner reminds us that these beings, however odious their presence,
cannot be eliminated. It is crucial, however, especially since these forces
tend to rebel against the cosmic order and to inappropriately influence
the sphere of human activities, that they be kept in balance. For when
they overstep their cosmic legitimacies, Lucifer and Ahriman instigate
evil, thereby negating the possibilities for freedom and perverting the
inherent meaning of love.

Steiner's many references to Lucifer and Ahriman allow us to appreciate these spirit-beings' tasks in orienting human souls to the becoming
and decaying between the world of the physical senses and the world of
the spirit. Lucifer's world-task consists in preventing human souls from
binding themselves exclusively to the sense world. If Lucifer were to
undertake this mission correctly, his influence would assist human souls
to develop creatively and to minimize the suffering brought about by the
brute reality of physical existence through artistic and religious endeavors. As a result, the soul would have developed feelings of gratitude and
responsibility for the earth. Lucifer, however, refuses this mission. The
Luciferic deviation consists primarily in making feeling independent from
thinking, and in retarding the soul's power to perceive and participate in
the physical world in a way that is commensurate with the progressive
evolution of consciousness. Keeping the soul enthralled with spiritual
realms and practices that are suited to ancient times, Lucifer instills the
soul with attitudes that breed illusion, false idealism, and fanaticism.

Ahriman's world-task consists in regulating the forces of death in
the physical world. The correct Ahrimanic influence would assist human
souls in attaining knowledge of death and in overcoming the fear of the
end of physical life. As a result, the soul would have recognized death
as a passing event that begins a return to the spiritual origin. Ahriman,

however, refuses this mission; the Ahrimanic deviation consists primarily in accelerating the soul's positive evaluation of and obsession with the physical world in a way that threatens the progressive evolution of consciousness. By promoting a form of thinking that yokes the soul to the methods of materialist science, and by providing the allure of ever new technologies that provide immediate gratifications, including the promise of immortality, Ahriman speeds up the processes of death and degeneration while denying the existence of a spiritual world.

Through their deviations, both these spirit-beings contribute to the growth of evil: Lucifer, by intoxicating the soul so that it becomes unable to distinguish its inherent creativity from delusion; Ahriman, by densifying the soul so that it becomes unable to infuse its intellect with living thinking. As a consequence of the Luciferic and Ahrimanic deviations, human beings become more entrenched in egoism. Consequently, and unconsciously, as human beings become more and more inclined to identify the truth of being with the material world and with a form of subjectivity that is inseparable from the physical body, we become susceptible to the feeling that we are emptying and hollowing out. This distressing experience, which is commensurate with the sensation that something has stepped outside of our bodies, reveals that the Luciferic and Ahrimanic forces are intimately bound up with the age-old problem of the *double* (dopplegänger).

The phenomenon of the double, the alter ego or phantom mirror-image of the self, is not unique to esoteric thinkers. Bizarre, grotesque, and macabre figures of split consciousness are encountered in poetry, shamanic rites, and literature. The double is also a pervasive theme in psychoanalysis, written about by Freud, in his essay "The Uncanny" (1919), and Rank, in his book *The Double* (1925). In both of these works the double is explicated with reference to the neurosis of pathological self-love, the defensive, narcissistic fear of death that often leads to paranoid insanity. Jung (1975) amplifies this psychoanalytic understanding in his description of the Shadow archetype, which he posits as the structural repository for the unintegrated and unsavory aspects of the personality. He declares that the entire therapeutic endeavor is little more then an "apprenticeship" in dealing with the shadow.

In whatever genre it is portrayed, the double, whose form is spectral, gives presence to a visceral counterpart of the everyday ego. While the double is an apparition, it is not only a ghostly figure, but also a space-occupying being that can move or remain immobile, act, and even speak. Regardless of the form, a person perceiving a manifestation of the double knows that he is seeing himself in front of himself, and is duly shocked and frightened. It is possible, however, that the always unsettling experience of perceiving the double can become more for the soul than a momentary acknowledgement of the negative aspects of its personality. If perception of the double is to open the soul to its own "other self," to its "true I," then this phantom being must be understood as embodying the workings of spirit-beings, whether they originate in evolutionary processes or in members of the human being itself.

Steiner's spiritual understanding of the double encompasses many of its manifestations. He specifically addresses what can be called the universal collective double in a lecture given on November 16, 1917 (2004). Maintaining that the physical body of incarnation cannot be fully filled up by the soul, Steiner discloses that for a short time before we are born there exists the opportunity for a spiritual being to take possession of the subconscious part of our body-mind. According to Steiner, this spiritual being is the Ahrimanic double, which he characterizes as composed of an "extraordinarily high intelligence and a significantly developed will, but no warmth of heart at all, nothing of what we call human soul warmth (Gemut)." Accompanying our souls throughout life "below the threshold of consciousness," the Ahrimanic double uses the physical body to exist and act in the human sphere up to the event that it cannot endure: death. That the Ahrimanic double must leave the human body before death is a consequence of Christ passing through the Mystery of Golgotha. Without this world-altering experience of death and resurrection, Ahriman would have triumphed, conquering death in human nature and becoming master of human evolution on earth.

Steiner warns with great urgency that humanity must come to know this inner Ahrimanic double if it is to avoid "endless horrors." If left to its own devices, the Ahrimanic double, whose very strong will "is much more akin to the nature forces than our human will, which is regulated by the warmth of soul [*Gemut*]," will attempt to link all that concerns human beings to the forces that stream up out of the earth. From its intimate relationship to these forces, such as magnetism, electricity, and atomic energy, the Ahrimanic double works both to intensify the materialistic attitude of humanity and to tighten and rigidify the human etheric body (1997c, 75–96). The Ahrimanic double aims to achieve an incursion, not only into the nerve-sense processes, but even into the soul, that ultimately seeks to restrict thinking to calculation and planning. By continuously diminishing the vitality of the life forces, the further program of the Ahrimanic double is to actually prevent the soul from having any thoughts that could uncover the reality of the spiritual world. Consequently, Ahriman and the Ahrimanic double underlie all the forms that evil assumes in our fifth post-Atlantean epoch.

Alongside the universal collective Ahrimanic double, Steiner presents a double that is completely bound up with the single individual. In the lecture "Human Tasks in the Higher Worlds," from *At the Gates of Spiritual Science*, Steiner is concerned with the forces that contribute to a new incarnation. From his researches into the spiritual world, Steiner reports on life after death. He remarks that the dissolution of the astral corpse (that is, in Steiner's theory of the human body, the aspect that houses our wishes, longings, and desires) is contingent upon whether a person, in the life between birth and death, has worked on the tendency of the lower passions to consolidate egoism. For those persons who have been unwilling or unable to restrain their impulsivity and sexual aggression, "the process of dissolution goes slowly, [and] sometimes the earlier astral corpse is not wholly dissolved when its original bearer returns to a new birth." In these cases, the newly incarnating human being encounters remnants of the old, undissolved astral corpse. Additionally, because the newly created astral body is too immature to resist the process of combination, this person will be compelled to "drag both of them along throughout life." This process is far from stable, and the astral remains can easily become detached from the incarnate human being. They then reappear in the form of an individual double that provokes fearful dreams, irrational behavior, and the disposition of soul that is most characteristic of our time: manic-depression or bi-polar disorders.

In another lecture, given on January 29, 1912 (2004), Steiner describes what could be called the double of the future. Carrying out a meditative exercise creates this double, in which one surveys history with the goal of distinguishing between events that demonstrate "apparent chance and obvious necessity." Especially when considering "fortuitous happenings" that we seemingly did not wish for, Steiner instructs us to adopt an attitude whereby we picture "the possibility of having ourselves put forth a deliberate and strong effort of will in order to bring them about." This meditation awakens the impression that "something [is] striving to be released from us." As this mental image of a "second being" begins to connect to the soul in such a way that we realize that it actually exists within us, we perceive the forming of our double. With this meditative perception of the double, the soul not only recognizes that the apparently chance happenings of today are rooted in will impulses of the past, but also experiences the "conviction that we were already in existence before" this incarnation. In addition to awakening consciousness to the reality of repeated incarnations, a meditative encounter with the double supports the path of inner development that counters the Luciferic and Ahrimanic defilements of the inherent meaning of love. By expediting the arduous psychological work of taking responsibility for one's feelings of blame, pain, and shame, the meditative encounter with the double challenges the evil of egoism. Specifically, the meditative encounter with the double produces an inward metamorphosis of soul that finds expression in the quality of *selflessness*. Giving evidence that the ego has been attuned to and emptied of self-seeking by the admonition and cautioning of the conscience, selflessness reflects the attainment of self-consciousness as a knowledge of being—a knowledge that is accessible to all humanity and makes us aware that all who share a human countenance and possess language are equal.

Beyond this general form of self-consciousness, the soul quality of selflessness also discloses a higher form of knowledge: a knowledge whereby we attain consciousness of our self-consciousness and come to an awareness of an individual "feeling of Self." As a second form of conscience that inheres within the quality of selflessness, the "feeling of Self" guides our life not only from the fact and tasks of being, but also toward the realization of our undetermined potential for goodness. Often awakened by a transformative experience that constellates around the need to repent and to suspend judgment through practices of compassion, the "feeling of Self" is a call to take up our own destiny and unite ourselves with it. Conscious that this destiny is animated by the holy, we can, in selflessness, follow the call of conscience to confront the evils of dehumanization and terror with free acts of generosity and kindness, realizing the eternal and absolute value of love.

Heidegger

In their understanding of conscience as that which gives voice to the "holy," Steiner and Heidegger could have enjoyed a rich philosophical dialogue. Our understanding of Steiner's views gains depth when we consider that, for Heidegger, the experience of conscience comes through openness to *Being*—that central but "forgotten" question that animates the philosopher's entire oeuvre. By investigating the question of Being in Heidegger's terms, we further enable reverence to serve as a foundational attunement for the unfolding of a modern initiatic consciousness.

Heidegger declared that the recollection of the question of Being "must be sought in the *existential analytic of Dasein*" (BT 34). *Dasein*, the self-entity that inquires into the possibilities of its own Being—i.e., the one who can and must ask the forgotten question—comes, through the practical necessity of participating in everyday life, unavoidably into contact with the beings and objects of the world. It is through these involvements with the impersonal and neutral ensemble constituting the commerce and discourse of the everyday world, which Heidegger calls "the 'they'" (*das Man*) (BT 164), that *Dasein* constructs its being-in-the-world. This existential process, which results in a differentiation from others and a sinking into the "averageness" of everyday life, pulls *Dasein* into and away from the question of its own being, leading to its "subjection" to the "they."

Encouraging *Dasein's* absorption in the world of beings and things and exploiting its fascination with the details of life, the "they" insidiously distracts *Dasein* from attending to or accepting the option to be itself. In the closeness of public life, "every secret loses its force" (BT 165), and

Dasein's authentic possibility of noticing its own "being-there" is endangered by the covering up that is essential to the process of forgetting. Heidegger calls this mode of being-in-the-world, which he interprets as inauthentic, the "falling" of *Dasein* (BT 219).

Heidegger is careful to point out that this expression is not meant to communicate a negative judgment of the human condition, but simply to describe the manner in which *Dasein* comports its being-in-the-world in the domain of inauthentic everydayness. This movement of "temptation, tranquilizing, alienation and entanglement" constitutes for Heidegger a "downward plunge" (*Absturz*) of *Dasein* into its own Being (BT 221–23). Losing itself by thrusting itself into everyday "theyness," *Dasein* is sucked into a confused and unstable commotion that relentlessly rips apart its self-understanding and inhibits it from the projecting of authentic possibilities.

In considering how *Dasein* can return from its absorption in the ordinary everydayness of "they" and instead turn toward its authentic possibilities for being, Heidegger undertakes an interpretation that begins by differentiating between two ways in which *Dasein* discloses itself: fear and anxiety. According to Heidegger, the unique feature of fear is that it manifests a shrinking back from something that always comes from the external world. Fear is always "fear of" something exact and explicit. Anxiety, on the other hand, is indefinite, unspecific, and unattached to anything within the world. In fact, the oppressive and obstinate experience of anxiety, that it comes from and relates to "nowhere and nothing," reveals that *Dasein* is exposed to a realm of possibilities that exceed and underlie the realities of the object world. This realm is the world as such. Consequently, *Being-in-the-world itself is that in the face of which one has anxiety* (BT 231).

Anxiety throws *Dasein* back upon that which it is anxious about, its authentic potentiality for Being-in-the-world. In addition, anxiety makes apparent to *Dasein* its freedom to choose and realize itself, which is the same as the freedom to appropriate its individuality in a process of individuation. By making us feel "uncanny" or "not-at-home" (*unheimlich*) (BT 233), anxiety upsets the induced sedation and collapses the easy self-confidence promoted by being-at-home with the everyday concerns of the "they." Hence, *Dasein's* freedom and individualization are irrevocably marked by the uncanny discovery that in our very being-in-the-world we are undeniably not-at-home. When *Dasein*, or being-there, is most fully present *in the world* that serves as our home, it is least present *in Being*.

Since anxiety is always latent in Being-in-the-world, *Dasein* is always anxious in the very depths of its Being. Though that anxiety may be blunted by the entangling "fall" into public life or the self-medicating use of tranquilizers, its inescapability involves *Dasein* in a terrible irony: although human being is characterized by being-in-the-world, we are never at home in the world. Uncanniness, or being-not-at-home, is a fundamental feature of existence. As the foundation of our unremitting disquiet, which unsettles us whenever we encounter the powerful innocence, grace, and beauty that is the aliveness of life, uncanniness permeates those "moments of vision" (*Augenblick*) when we are truly inspired by awe (BT 376). Not surprisingly, it is also the uncanny experience of homelessness, as the ruinous reality of exile, that fills *Dasein* with apprehension and permits *Dasein* to apprehend at any moment its most extreme possibility for Being, namely, Being-toward-death.

When we are confronted with the reality of our death, we feel how inevitably it is our own. Death is "always essentially mine," the "ownmost possibility of *Dasein*" (BT 297). In extricating itself from its everyday fallenness, from the anonymity of the thought that "one dies," the dreaded anticipation of its death opens *Dasein* to grasping itself in its authenticity. To make this grasping a gesture toward healing and wholeness, *Dasein* must undergo a preliminary "attestation" of its being-its-Self and submit itself to the "voice of conscience" (*Stimme des Gewissen*), as a "call" (*Ruf*) (BT 313–17). Insinuating itself into the numbing noise of everydayness, where *Dasein* "*fails to hear [uberhort]* its own Self in listening to the they-self" (Ibid., 315), the voice of conscience directs *Dasein* toward acknowledging its "guilt," which is its finitude or constitutional limitedness, and choosing to accept its Self for what it is. With this recognition of vulnerability comes an unshakeable resolve that expresses a "readiness to be called." Consequently, the voice of conscience serves as a way for *Dasein* to achieve the authenticity that is proper to its Self.

Heidegger termed the kind of hearing the voice of conscience arouses in *Dasein* "receptive listening" (PLT 209). Obviously involved with priorities other than the clichés, slogans, and gossip of the "they," receptive listening not only distinguishes the primary way in which the Self can respond to the concerns of the external or internal other. It also gives *Dasein* access to the mode of discourse characteristic of calling, which Heidegger describes as "the uncanny mode of *keeping silent*" (BT 322). Saying nothing and remaining steadfastly non-communicative, this voice, speaking without sound or words, manages to track down *Dasein* and threaten the foreignness in which it has abandoned itself. Eschewing vagueness, the call arrives as a pure summons that "*manifests itself as the call of care.*" In other words, *Dasein*, in the very basis of its Being, is care (BT 322–23).

In his later writings, especially the essays that appear in *Poetry, Language, Thought* (PLT), *Elucidations of Hölderlin's Poetry* (EHP), and *On the Way to Language* (OWL), Heidegger examines the call of conscience in terms of *language*. Displacing the uncanny sense of homelessness that haunts our being-in-the-world from birth toward death, he situates our homecoming in the revelatory powers of poetry. To understand this transference, we must realize that the call of conscience functions as a bulwark against the dangers of technology. What is most radical in Heidegger's analysis is his claim that the essential danger of technicity is not the way the sheer availability and wide-ranging usage of technological devices make an increasingly exclusive claim upon our perception and behavior. Nor is it that technology warps and replaces the decisive differentiation involved in coming to presence by building objective presence into everything, including the subject. Rather, the danger is in the way technicity entails and arranges permanent crisis as the defining condition of the modern world. As the inescapable determination of our era, technicity operates as an "enframing" [*Gestell*] or negative fusing that pushes relentlessly toward domination.

More worrisome, the fundamental attitude of technicity, which reduces all beings, including ourselves, to quantifiable resources always ready for use and possibly abuse, easily merges with the "universalization of terror," which advances the dissolution of any way to qualitatively measure the true or discern the real. As a counter to this dissolution, Heidegger poses conscience as the mode of care whereby we heed the call to shelter the precarious relation between Being and beings and to protect the fragile possibility of a reconciliation between humans and nature. He advocates a "doing for the sake of doing" that emanates from an individual's own value system, developed independently of the "they." Such an individual, he suggests, might uniquely subvert technicity's demand for effectiveness and productivity by engaging instead in "essential or meditative" thinking, allowing herself to become permeated by what Heidegger calls "releasement toward things" (*Die Gelassenheit zu den Dingen*) and "openness to the mystery"(DT 54).

In light of his decades-long consideration of the work of Hölderlin, it is hardly surprising that Heidegger's name for these rare individuals who can meditatively question technicity is *poet*. Drawn to the authentic use or Saying capacity of language, which is the "primal event" that grants us the "possibility of standing in the midst of the openness of beings" (EHP 56), the poet is favored with a venturesome daring which demands non-ordinary experiences. These extraordinary experiences orient poetry toward "that chaos… out of which the open opens itself." The originary openness that Heidegger associates with Holderlin's primal chaos also signifies for him "the holy itself" (EHP 85).

The Holy is primordial. Remaining eternally All That Is, the Holy is always unbroken and forever undefiled. As originary wholeness, the Holy is absolutely ultimate. As the Source from which All That Is can appear or withdraw, the Holy is the dimension where the truth of Being tends to hide. Because it is "im-mediate," prior to any and all mediations that establish relations between beings, the Holy is only indirectly accessible to gods and humans alike. Abiding in itself as the groundless ground of all experience, "the Holy is the awesome itself" (Ibid.).

Anticipating the crucial question of whether an experience of the Holy is possible within the world of technicity, let us consider the poet, whose unique destiny is to receive a direct call from the Holy. Accepting and welcoming the call, the poet is tasked to respond. Cultivating response-ability, which is by definition a gesture of conscience, entails a subordination of the self-assertive, egoistic will. From this step backwards, which Heidegger terms "reservedness" (CP 12; 24), the poet's response enhances the predisposition to find in her Self the level of conscious-ness that psycho-spiritual schooling calls the interior world of the "pure heart" (EHP 93). Abiding reservedly with pure-heart consciousness, the poet realizes that she is more than a human but less than a god—that she dwells in a rarefied environment in between ordinary humanity and divinity. Living in intimate connection with the interior world of the pure heart, the poet displays the calm preparedness that waits to be addressed by "the gods who have failed to arrive" (PLT 91).

When the absent god or gods approaches the poet, and by lightning flash or thundering voice finally awakens her from silence, she is granted an originating *logos* that gives rise to her *word*. Receiving this gift as one from a time that is "not yet," the poet does not ascribe the *logos* to her own credit; instead she heartily affirms that what has been sent is a manifestation of the awesome and of the yet "to come." Submitting to the negativity (self-concealment) of the Holy in order to become the messenger of the *logos*, the poet knows she has been given the source of what she must bring into words. Serving her only true concern, which is to protect the manifold ways in which the mystery of Being is conceived and to announce its advent, the poet is called to give an authentic utter-ance. As a result of heeding the demands of Being in good conscience, the very heart and soul of the poet become centered in "the quietness of their belonging within the embrace of the holy" (EHP 93).

It cannot be too strongly emphasized that the poet's attainment of homecoming within the embrace of the Holy has nothing to do with her own creativity or subjectivity. Nor is it a matter of good or ill fortune. Rather, the embrace by the Holy rests upon the unknown destiny that unfolds as the event of Being.

With this assertion, I return to the question of Being, which is always Heidegger's essential and only question. At this time and in a world dominated by the priorities of technicity, turning toward the question of Being means questing after a renewal of conscience and the recovery of our lost feeling-sense for the Holy. It is the poet's task to prepare us for a new openness to the Holy, in which the divine can be spoken about without reference to a highest being, so that through this inspired speaking we may come to "dwell poetically" (PLT 211)—to live carefully and peacefully with the beings and things of the earth. In addition, "to 'dwell poetically' means to stand in the presence of the gods and to be struck by the nearness of things" (EHP 60). Consequently, to make dwelling poetically possible, human beings must learn to dwell near the truth of Being.

In our time of need, which Heidegger calls "a destitute time" (PLT 142), learning to dwell near the truth of Being means that each of us must activate the capacity for becoming poetic that was once the privilege of the poets. On the level of everydayness, one way of becoming poetic is opening to the essence of language, which means refusing to regard language as a material object for our disposal and realizing that the authentic use of language, prior even to communication, is conversation. Becoming poetic also means that conversation surpasses the mere exchange of information and instead gives voice to a speaking that is intrinsically musical, rhythmic, and inconstant, and to an individuality that is inherently improvisational, goalless, and pliant.

On the level of authentic conversation, poetry is a naming of Being. In addition, since authentic conversation names the Holy as the place where the gods can appear, however provisionally, becoming poetic satisfies this Holy need: "The poets first lay out and secure the building site upon which the house must be built in which the gods are to come as guests" (EHP 170). Moreover, because becoming poetic means accepting that humans are always already situated in and addressed by language, letting ourselves find the *logos* that rightly attunes our conscience helps us to overcome the uncanny sense of homelessness that corresponds to the absence of the Holy.

While the loss of a feeling-sense for the Holy is perhaps the most pressing threat that characterizes the age of technicity, it remains secondary to and enveloped in the question of Being. Since we must learn to dwell near the truth of Being in order to live in a historical and contemporary relation to the gods— a task that comes with the evolution of freedom—becoming poetic facilitates the transformation whereby humans must become *Dasein*. Offering somewhat enigmatic guidance as to the nature of this transformation, Heidegger teaches, "Be-ing holds sway [unfolds] as the 'between' [*Zwischen*] for god and man, but in such a way that this between-space [*Zwischenraum*] first grants essential possibility for god and man…" (CP 335).

The essential condition that emerges from the subtle space of the between is the *possible* or the not-yet-real, which Heidegger prioritizes over the real (EHP 136). Moreover, it is the possible that demands of us the maturation of conscience whereby we can receptively listen to the hints dimly offered in the speech of the passing gods before speaking of the coming or return of the Holy. Since "Be-ing holds sway [unfolds] as needfulness of god in the guardianship of *Dasein*" (CP 341), this advent of the Holy as the abode of the gods only approaches in response to our attempting the daring venture of conscience through which we, as human beings, become *Dasein*. This becoming unfolds primarily by resisting acquiescence to the "enframing" of technicity and through practicing non-attachment to all ordinary and known understandings of *humanism*. In the daring venture of conscience, we facilitate the clearing necessary for ourselves to serve as the site of the "t/here" (*Da*) that protects Being (*Sein*) from being identified with any being and shelters Being from obliteration by the terror that is technicity.

Conclusion

Irradiated by the golden ray of the gods, aware that the Infinite is already present in everything finite, and contained in a "light embrace" of the awesome, Heidegger's "future poets" are educated to know the Holy. They have been educated not from afar but in the firmness and the intimacy of the "eternal heart," and they know the Holy as the "initiated ones" (EHP 85). Identifying initiatic knowledge with "divination," the future poets, who stand between men and gods and are "essentially 'spiritual' themselves" (EHP 86), are also the poets *of the future*.

Although able to divine the dawning of the open realm from which there shines out the light that is the life of the spirit, the poets of the future are unable "to say who He himself is who dwells in the holy, and in saying this to let him appear as himself" (EHP 45). This deficiency is not a fault of the poets, nor does it suggest any insufficiency of the *logos*. Rather, the "holy names" are lacking and the god remains absent/ distant because an undeniable and seemingly unbridgeable schism exists between our consciousness and our conscience. This destructive rupture between our perceptual awareness and our faculty of moral judgment reflects materialism's largely successful effort to convince us that the death of the Judeo-Christian God relativizes the essential truth of Being and relegates the spiritual world to the realm of superstition. Moreover, this split provokes the spread of a virulent egoism which threatens to eclipse any appreciation for goodness and discourage deeds of altruistic or empathic sacrifice. This psychic fissuring causes a hardening of our souls, and it falls to the poets, those whose historic role is to give voice to the Holy by serving as the "there" [*Da*] between humans and the gods, to undertake healing ventures.

If her efforts are to save the future of humanity from paralyzing dissociation and susceptibility to both sadistic and masochistic enactments of violence, the poet must resist finding comfort in traditional theologies and archaic mystical practices that neglect or exclude expansion toward the mystery of an unknown destiny. She must also refrain from resorting to those temporary forms of transcendence (often spontaneous or chemically induced) which avoid confronting the "double/shadow" as intrinsic to the painful earthly path of coming to self-knowledge, and reject the "enlightened belief" that the evil does not exist. Meeting these preliminary conditions, the poet strengthens conscience, the inner creative source that bestows individuality; she also encourages us to contest injustice, and promotes healthy transformation in herself and others.

If, however, the poet is to prefigure the way we can consciously stand "in" the light of Being (Source/Holy), then she must both articulate and personify the renunciation of the willful quest for constant presence that is the hallmark of technicity and a bedrock of the universalization of terror. This act of detachment from the will is the beginning of a mutation of the will: from will to power to will as letting. "When we let ourselves into releasement to that-which-regions, we will non-willing" (DT 79). Turning toward the open expanse where our non-willing yet heartfelt commitment to conscience unfolds, the poet turns us all toward the quest for self-knowledge that would reveal what has always remained obscure or concealed in "the mystery" [*das Geheimnis*].

For a model of how to open to this mystery, we can turn to what Rudolf Steiner identified as the pivotal mystery of human life: the Mystery of Golgotha. Thus from Heidegger's impersonal Being we can turn to the Christ as the living, spiritual being whose incarnation is the experience of overcoming and becoming. Or, to recall Nietzsche, Christ is an example of the nobility of soul that transcends the challenges we all meet as spirits incarnated in human bodies.

In the lecture series *From Jesus to Christ*, Steiner declares that the Christ Event in Palestine effected a translation and enhancement of the act and meaning of initiation. I think it would be fair to say that Steiner characterizes the transformation of initiation brought about by Christ's experience of death and resurrection as a process of unprecedented importance: the deregulation of "what had formerly been carried out on a small scale in the depths of the Mysteries was now once and for all enacted for humanity by Divine Spirits, and that the Being who is designated as the Father acted as hierophant in the raising to life of Christ Jesus" (1973b, 105).

Thus the Event of Golgotha brought something to human evolution that is both restorative and generative. In giving us the gift of his Body, Christ overcame the corruptible Adamic Body (the physical human body, with its inherited inability to counter the destructive Luciferic forces) by liberating the Resurrection Body, or the Phantom, the spiritual archetype of the human being. At Christ's death, his Phantom descended into the abyss of the earth, where he united with and defeated Ahriman. Hence with this sacrifice he triumphed over the dark powers we all must face, strengthening us in turn to rise toward and participate in the spiritual world.

As an initiatic model of the renunciation of egoism, the life and death of Jesus demonstrated the separation of the physical body from the eternal Christ Spirit. It would therefore betray a misunderstanding of the nature of the Christ Being to expect a Second Coming in the flesh; instead, Steiner spoke of "the reappearance of Christ in the etheric." Since the Event at Golgotha, we are called not to passively wait for grace, but to strive for the freedom in self-awareness through which we gain access to our home in the spiritual world. It is on the higher etheric plane, dwelling as the Lord of Karma (Ibid. 170), that Christ supports the growth of new affective-cognitive capacities that enhance our moral imagination, giving us courage to overcome the shame of suffering and the guilt of causing pain. Insofar as Christ awakens our souls, we too become able to spiritualize our physical and supersensible bodies.

When Christ's blood dripped into the earth, we were liberated to realize, through a free and conscious act, the divine spark or seed living in every human being. In this deliberate act the modern initiate gains independence and sovereignty over the desires and habits of her ego-body and the sabotages of her various doubles or shadow figures—not through fusion or renunciation, but through the love and wisdom of her "I"-consciousness or higher Self. Aware of the tempting lures of evil, but dedicated to the noble virtues of beauty, goodness, and truth, the modern initiate transforms herself from a calculating and acquisitive being into a kind and bestowing one, from a being reliant on the generosity and favors of others to a source of generosity and favor *for* others.

Identifying contemporary spiritual knowledge and practice with Christ's personification of infinite love and repeated sacrifice, the modern initiate undertakes the sacred work of countering the ongoing dehumanization of humanity, the potential destruction of the planet, and the onset of a cosmic night wrought by the unholy merger between universalized terror and evil. She knows in the depths of her heart that she must embody this practice and that countering this negativity is the joyous affirmation of her destiny and her dignity as a human being. And so she does.

Literature Cited

Abraham, Nicolas, and Maria Torok. 1994. *The Shell and the Kernel*. Vol. 1. Translated by Nicholas T. Rand. Chicago: University of Chicago Press.

Bataille, Georges. 1985. *Visions of Excess*. Translated by Allan Stoekl. Minneapolis: University of Minnesota Press.

Bion, W. R. 1965. *Transformations*. London: Maresfield.

_____. 1967. *Second Thoughts*. London: Karnac Books.

_____. 1970. *Attention and Interpretation*. London: Karnac Books.

_____. 1983. *Learning from Experience*. New York: Jason Aronson.

_____. 1992. *Cogitations*. London: Karnac Books.

Bromberg, Philip M. 1998. *Standing in the Spaces*. New York: The Analytic Press.

Eliade, Mircea. 1959. *The Sacred and the Profane*. Translated by Willard R. Trask. New York: Harcourt, Brace & World.

Estrada, Alvaro. 1981. *Maria Sabina: Her Life and Chants*. Translated by Henry Munn. Santa Barbara: Ross-Erikson Inc.

Freud, S. 1948. "The Uncanny." In *Collected Papers*, Vol. 4, London: Hogarth Press.

_____. 1962. *Civilization and Its Discontents*. Translated by James Strachey. New York: W. W. Norton & Company.

Grof, Stanislav. 1988. *The Adventure of Self-Discovery*. Albany: SUNY Press.

Grotstein, James. 1995. "Bion's 'Transformation in "O"' and the 'Transcendent Position.'" In *A Beam of Intense Darkness*. London: Karnac Books, 2007.

Harner, Michael (editor). *Hallucinogens and Shamanism*. London: Oxford University Press.

Heidegger, Martin. 1962a. *Being and Time*. Translated by John Macquarrie and Edward Robinson. New York: Harper& Row.

_____. 1962b. "Letter on 'Humanism.'" Translated by Edgar Lohner. In Barrett, William, and Henry D. Aiken, eds. *Philosophy in the Twentieth Century*. New York: Random House.

_____. 1966. *Discourse on Thinking*. Translated by John M. Anderson and E. Hans Freund. New York: Harper& Row.

_____. 1968. *What Is Called Thinking?* Translated by J. Glenn Grey and Fred Wieck. New York: Harper& Row.

_____. 1971. *Poetry, Language, Thought.* Translated by Albert Hofstadter. New York: Harper& Row.

_____. 1973. *The End of Philosophy.* Translated by Joan Stambaugh. New York: Harper& Row.

_____. 1977. *The Question Concerning Technology and Other Essays.* Translated by William Lovitt. New York: Harper& Row.

_____. 1984. *Nietzsche.* Vol. 2, "The Eternal Recurrence of the Same." Translated by David Farrell Krell. San Francisco: Harper & Row.

_____. 1994. *Basic Questions of Philosophy.* Translated by Richard Rojcewicz and Andre Schuwer. New York: Harper& Row.

_____. 1999. *Contributions to Philosophy (From Enowning).* Translated by Parvis Emad and Kenneth Maly. Bloomington: Indiana University Press.

_____. 2000. *Elucidations of Hölderlin's Poetry.* Translated by Keith Hoeller. Amherst, New York: Humanity Books.

_____. 2006. *Mindfulness.* Translated by Parvis Emad and Thomas Kalary. New York: Continuum.

Jung, C. G. 1966. *The Psychology of the Transference* (CW 16). Princeton: Princeton University Press.

_____. 1969. "Psychological Commentary on *The Tibetan Book of the Great Liberation.*" In *Psychology and Religion: West and East.* Princeton: Princeton University Press.

_____. 1975. *Aion.* CW 9, ii. Princeton: Princeton University Press.

_____. 1988. *Nietzsche's Zarathustra.* Translated by James L. Jarrett. Princeton: Princeton University Press.

Krell, David Farrell. 1992. *Daimon Life.* Bloomington: Indiana University Press.

Kühlewind, Georg. 1983. *Feeling Knowing.* Translated by Friedemann Schwarzkopf. Fair Oaks, California: Rudolf Steiner College Press.

_____. 1984. *Stages of Consciousness.* Translated by Michael Lipson. Great Barrington, Massachusetts.: Lindisfarne Press.

_____. 1987. *Thinking of the Heart and Other Essays.* Fair Oaks, California: Rudolf Steiner College Press.

_____. 1988. *From Normal to Healthy.* Translated by Michael Lipson. Hudson, New York: Lindisfarne Press.

_____. 1990. *The Life of the Soul.* Translated by Michael Lipson. Hudson, New York: Lindisfarne Press.

Lampert, L. 1986. *Nietzsche's Teaching*. New Haven: Yale University Press.

McKenna, Terence. 1992. *Food of the Gods*. New York: Bantam Books.

Nietzsche, Friedrich. 1961. *Thus Spoke Zarathustra*. Translated by R. J. Hollingdale. Penguin Books.

_____. 1968. *The Anti-Christ*. Translated by R. J. Hollingdale. Penguin Books.

_____. 1973. *Beyond Good and Evil*. Translated by R. J. Hollingdale. Penguin Books.

_____. 1974. *The Gay Science*. Translated by Walter Kaufmann. Penguin Books.

_____. 1979. *Ecce Homo*. Translated by R. J. Hollingdale. Penguin Books.

Ott, Jonathan. 1997. *Pharmacophilia or the Natural Paradises*. Kennewick, Washington: Natural Products Co.

Otto, Rudolf. 1976. *The Idea of the Holy*. London: Oxford University Press.

Plato. 1973. *The Collected Dialogues*. Princeton: Princeton University Press.

Prokofieff, Sergei O. 1994. *Rudolf Steiner and the Founding of the New Mysteries*. London: Temple Lodge Publishing.

_____. 2004. *The Occult Significance of Forgiveness*. Temple Lodge Publishing.

Rank, Otto. 1971. *The Double: A Psychoanalytic Study*. Trans. and edited by Harry Tucker Jr. Chapel Hill: University of North Carolina Press.

Sardello, Robert. 1999. *Freeing the Soul from Fear*. New York: Riverhead Books.

_____. 2006. *Silence*. Benson, North Carolina: Goldenstone Press.

Schuré, Edouard. 1970. *From Sphinx to Christ*. San Francisco: Harper & Row.

Schwartz-Salant, Nathan. 2007. *The Black Nightgown: The Fusional Complex and the Unlived Life*. Wilmette, Illinois: Chiron Publications.

Stambaugh, Joan. 1994. *The Other Nietzsche*. Albany: SUNY Press.

Steiner, Rudolf. 1941. *The Challenge of the Times*. Spring Valley, New York: Anthroposophic Press.

_____. 1966. *Occult Science and Occult Development*. London: Rudolf Steiner Press.

_____. 1972. *Building Stones for an Understanding of the Mystery of Golgotha*. London: Rudolf Steiner Press.

_____. 1973a. *Anthroposophical Leading Thoughts*. London: Rudolf Steiner Press.

_____. 1973b. *From Jesus to Christ*. London: Rudolf Steiner Press.

_____. 1974. *Awakening to Community*. Spring Valley, New York: Anthroposophic Press.

_____. 1983a. *The Reappearance of Christ in the Etheric*. Spring Valley, New York: Anthroposophic Press.

_____. 1983b. *Metamorphosis of the Soul*. Vol. 2. London: Rudolf Steiner Press.

_____. 1987. *The Secrets of the Threshold*. London: Rudolf Steiner Press.

_____. 1988. *The New Spirituality and the Christ Experience of the Twentieth Century*. Hudson, New York: Anthroposophic Press.

_____. 1990. *Psychoanalysis & Spiritual Psychology*. Hudson, New York: Anthroposophic Press.

_____. 1992. *Reincarnation and Karma*. Hudson, New York: Anthroposophic Press.

_____. 1993. *The Influences of Lucifer and Ahriman*. Hudson, New York: Anthroposophic Press.

_____. 1994a. *How to Know Higher Worlds*. Hudson, New York: Anthroposophic Press.

_____. 1994b. *The Archangel Michael*. Hudson, New York: Anthroposophic Press.

_____. 1995a. *Intuitive Thinking as a Spiritual Path*. Translated by Michael Lipson. Hudson, New York: Anthroposophic Press.

_____. 1995b. *Manifestations of Karma*. London: Rudolf Steiner Press.

_____. 1995c. *Anthroposophy in Everyday Life*. Hudson, New York: Anthroposophic Press.

_____. 1997a. *An Outline of Esoteric Science*. Hudson, New York: Anthroposophic Press.

_____. 1997b. *The Effects of Esoteric Development*. Hudson, New York: Anthroposophic Press.

_____. 1997c. *Evil*. London: Rudolf Steiner Press.

_____. 1998. *Love and Its Meaning in the World*. Hudson, New York: Anthroposophic Press.

_____. 2004. *Secret Brotherhoods*. London: Rudolf Steiner Press.

_____. 2005. *Start Now!* Great Barrington, Massachusetts: SteinerBooks.

_____. 2006. *Approaching the Mystery of Golgotha*. Great Barrington, Massachusetts: SteinerBooks.

Steiner, Rudolf, and Friedrich Benesch. 2001. *Reverse Ritual: Spiritual Knowledge Is True Communion*. Great Barrington, Massachusetts: Anthroposophic Press.

Tuncel, Yunus. 2006. *Zarathustra in Nietzsche's Typology*. www.nietzschecircle.com

Turner, Victor. 1982. *From Ritual to Theatre*. New York City: Performing Arts Journal Publications.

Wasson, R. Gordon. 1971. *Soma: Divine Mushroom of Immortality*. New York: Harcourt Brace Jovanovich.

_____. 1978. *The Road to Eleusis*. New York: Harcourt Brace Jovanovich.

Winnicott, D.W. 1971. *Playing and Reality*. London: Penguin Books.

Index

abandonment of being, 9
Adamic Body, 148
Adouizur, 21
Aeschylus, 130
Ahriman, 21-22, 101-105, 134-137, 148
  as spiritual being of darkness, 21
  as the double, 136-137
ahrimanic, 101-103, 107, 134-136, 138
Anaximander, 111
angel, 12-13
antipathies, 34, 55, 76, 98-99
anthroposophy, 11, 15, 66, 88, 96, 104, 111
anthroposophic psychology, 80, 85, 107-108
an unknown destiny, 4, 8, 14, 35, 104, 108, 144, 147
anxiety, 9, 140
archetypal, xxiv
archetypal imagination. *See* imagination, archetypal
art of style, 31
Asjabr. See Zarathustra
astral, 84, 137
astral body, 76-77, 80
atavistic, xv, 42. *See* also clairvoyance/clairvoyant
Atlantis, 111
  the flood, 130
attention deficit disorder, xx, 128
attentive presence, xviii
awe, 5, 141

Bataille, Georges, 26
  Visions of Excess, 26
Becoming, xix-xx, 33, 40, 59, 84
becoming-into-being. *See* Becoming
Being, xiv, xviii, xxii-xxiii, 8-11, 45, 109-110, 119, 121, 123-126, 129, 139-148

being-in-the-world, 2, 139, 141-142
being-not-at-home, 140-141
being-towards-death, 142
Bhagavad Gita, 42
Bion, W. R., 94-96
  concept of container/contained, 96
  intuitive attention, 95-96
  "O," the Transcendent Other, 95-96
  psychotherapeutic conversation, 84, 94-95
bi-polar disorder, xx, 137
blame, 57, 99
blessedness, 62
Bolshevik Revolution, 75
Bromberg, Philip, 72-73
  Standing in the Spaces, 72-73

centering heart, 87
chakras, 43
Christ, 11-13, 66-68, 103, 136, 148-149
  as Ahura-Mazda, 21
  His becoming, 62
  as a being of a higher order, 11
  en-Christened, 108
  as Cosmic Creator, 42
  as an enlightened being, 61
  as etheric, 13, 148
  incarnation, 67
  as Lord of Karma, 149
  Resurrection, 67, 136
  Resurrection Body, 148
  sacrificial deed, 11
  second coming, 12, 67, 148
  as Solar Spirit, 20, 42
  as Son, 62
  as spiritual light of the cosmos, 66
  transfiguration, 67
Christ consciousness, 107

Christ Impulse, 11
Christianity, 59
clairvoyance/clairvoyant, xxii, 53, 69, 75, 84, 88-89, 103, 130-131
cognition/cognitive, 11, 13, 22, 51, 69, 74, 91, 95, 105, 117-119, 130, 149
affective cognition, 12
compassion, 58, 83, 92, 94, 98, 106
concepts, 114-115, 117
individualized, 115
conceptual, 114
conscience, 25, 53, 58, 60, 113, 129, 131-132, 138-139, 141-142, 145, 146-147
consciousness, xiii-xiv, xvi-xviii, xxi, xxiii-xxiv, 1, 5, 7, 14-15, 22, 24, 26, 28, 36-37, 42, 46-47, 50, 63, 67-68, 70, 72, 74-75, 77-78, 84-86, 88-89, 91-93, 95, 97, 103, 108, 110-111, 113, 116-118, 129-130, 134-136, 138, 144, 147
centers of, 43
clairvoyant, 53
dualistic, xxiii
egoic, xiii-xiv, 24
imaginal, xvi-xviii
initiate/initiatic, xxi, 68, 89, 109-111, 118-119, 126, 139
intellectual, 75
materialistic, xviii
meditative, xv
modern (new), xx, 12
moral, 25, 118, 128, 130, 132
old, xxiii
pure heart, 144
shamanic, 47
soul, 129-130
spiritual, 104
split, 135
terroristic, xxiii
consciousness soul, 113, 119
contemplation, state of, 26
cosmic
being, 123, 125
cosmic-human, 54, 65
love, 35, 54
force, 35
"I," 74
image, 12
legitimacies, 134

life, 130
love, 89
mysteries, 37, 130
night, 149
order, 134
task, 13
cosmos, xvii, 23, 28, 44, 46, 66, 75, 118, 123, 129-130
countering, 11
cleverness cannot be countered, xxi
as a spiritual pathology, xxi

"Daimon-Life," 131
darkness, forces of, xviii
"death of God," 12-13, 18, 33, 41-42, 147
demonized, 73, 103
Descartes, 112
Dasein, 139-142, 145-146
destiny, xiii, 4, 8, 14, 35, 48, 103, 139, 147, 149,
dissociation/dissociative, 70, 73, 80, 82-83, 88, 127
Divine, the, 101, 103
Divine Silence, 2-3
as logos, 3
Divine Spirits, 148
double, (dopplegänger), 135-136. See also ego, alter ego
Ahrimanic, 136-137
double of the future (our double), 138
as soul's other self, 136
universal double, 136
doubling, xx-xxi
dragon slaying of, 12-13
dualism, 112
dwelling, xxiii, 9, 11

Earth, xxii-xxiv, 2, 23, 42, 75, 103, 129-130, 134, 137
ego ("I"), 3, 30, 34-36, 54, 57, 68, 76, 84-85, 87-88, 97, 104, 110, 113-115, 117, 132, 136, 138, 147
alter ego (double), 38-39
as "I"-Am, 85, 116-119
as individuality, xiii
as individuality of being, xiv
as self, xiii, 34-35, 49, 65, 69-70, 73-74, 76, 79, 85, 87, 98, 100, 114, 135, 138,

141-142
spiritual-"I," 80, 84-87
true or originary "I," 116-117, 136
ego-body, 149
ego-centeredness, 65, 87
ego-identity, 78
ego-psychology, 6
egoic/egoism, xiv, xxiii, 5, 12, 37, 54, 64-
65, 77, 88, 92, 97, 99, 101, 107, 110,
113, 125-126, 132-133, 135, 137-138,
143, 147-148
evil as egoism, 133
egotized, xx
Einstein, 75
elective affinity, 97
Eleusis, Dionysian rituals, 46
Eliade, Mircea, 46, 132
The Sacred and the Profane, 46, 132
elitism, 29
encounter, 107
enframing, 10, 142, 146
entheogens, 46, 48, 50. See also God
generated within
envy, 44
epochs, post-Atlantean cultural, 111
as seven wisdom epochs, 130
Ancient Indian, 42, 111
Ancient Persian, 111
Greco-Roman, 111, 130-131
modern (present), 1, 14, 36, 54, 74, 77,
85, 90-91, 97-98, 107, 112-113, 130,
137
etheric, 13, 104-105, 149
etheric body, 69, 76-77, 80, 84, 104-105
as subtle body, 77
etheric clairvoyance, 74, 108
evolution, xxi-xxii
exigency to creativity, 3

faith, 13, 67
fatalism, 57
fate, 33, 36, 51
fear, xiv, 14, 26, 51, 58, 63, 99, 140
feeling, xvii, xxiv, 24, 77-78, 80, 91, 98-99,
107, 114-118, 132, 134
feeling impression, 5
feeling of self, 139
forgiveness, 2, 57-58

freedom, xix, 1, 12, 15, 18, 33, 36, 60, 67-
68, 75, 78, 88, 90, 93, 104, 113, 123,
125, 132, 134, 140-141, 145, 149
freedom from purpose, 44
Freud, Sigmund, 2, 12, 75, 94
Civilization and Its Discontents, 2
Psychology Commentary, 5
The Uncanny, 135
Furies, 130

Gay Science, 1
gemstones, xxii
as a sacrifice of angelic beings, xxii
Gemut (inner soul warmth), 13, 15, 136-
137
God, xvii-xviii, 1, 7, 63, 103, 107, 112, 147
as Divine, 35
as Divine Other, 6
as Father, 62, 148
as Supreme Being, 1
God generated within, 46, 48. *See also*
entheogens
Golgotha, 66, 148
grace, 8, 109, 149
gravitation/gravity, 18, 20-22, 24-25, 27-
29, 31-33, 36-37, 41-42, 50, 75, 127
Greek culture, 2
Grof, Stanislav,
The Adventure of Self-Discovery, 28
Grotstein, James,
"Bion's 'Transformation in "O"' and the
'Trancendent Position,'" 95
Harner, Michael,
Hallucinations and Shamanism, 47
heart, (human), xviii, xxi, 124
heart-centeredness, 87-88
heart-thinking, xvi-xix, 5-6, 12, 54, 56,
59, 65, 67, 119
Hebraic, culture, 103
Heidegger, Martin, xv, xxi-xxiii, 4, 6, 8-
10, 15, 40, 45, 109-110, 119-125, 129-
130, 139-148
Basic Questions of Philosophy, 4, 65
Being and Time, 9, 129, 139-142
Beyond Good and Evil, 22
Contributions to Philosophy, 9-10, 144,
146
Discourse on Thinking, 10, 120-124

Elucidations of Holderlin's Poetry, 142-144, 146
End of Philosophy, 9
his esoteric philosophy, 8, 11
his lecture, "Gelassenheit," 119
the "Holy," 139, 143-147
Letter on Humanism, 9, 109
Mindfulness, 10
Nietzsche, 40
On the Way to Language, 142
Poetry, Language, Thought, 9, 109, 126, 142-144
"releasement toward things," 122-123
What Is Called Thinking? 110, 111
Heraclitus, 111
Hierarchies, 103
   Divine, 130
Hölderlin, 143
homecoming, 50
homelessness, 9, 145
human-world, xxi-xxii

"I." *See* ego
"I"-body, 78-79
"I"-consciousness, 65, 93, 115-117, 125, 149
   as higher self, 149
"I"-experience, 93
I-World, xxi
images, xxiv
imaginal consciousness. *See* consciousness, imaginative
imaginal perception, 26
imagination/imaginative, xiv-xv, xxii, 5, 36, 70-71, 80, 87, 89, 95, 104-106, 109
   archetypal, xx
   cognitions, 87-88
   prototypal, xx
   spiritual, xxi
impressions, xx, 5
India, ancient, 46-47
   their goddess of birth, 47
   their goddess of creation, 47
   their wisdom, 42-43, 46
individuality. *See* ego, individuality
individuation, process of, 14, 44, 107, 140-141
initiate consciousness. *See* consciousness,

initiate
initiation/initiatic/initiatory, xiv-xvi, xix-xxi, 3, 5, 12, 15, 19, 21-24, 28, 30-31, 36-38, 85, 129, 146, 148
   modern, xiv, xxiv, 3-5, 8, 11, 39, 66
   Persian, 22
   self-initiation, xiv
   therapeutic, xix, xxiv, 85
   world, xxi
inspiration, 5, 11, 50, 107, 145
instinct for rank, 30
interactive field, xix
interfacial region. *See* Winnecott, his interfacial region
internalization through sacrifice, 19
intuition/intuitive, xvii, xxii, 21, 33, 45, 50, 52, 59, 65, 73, 75, 86, 88, 92-93, 95-96, 107, 114-117, 125-126
intuitively seeing into, 73

Jekyl and Hyde phenomenon, xxi
Jesus of Nazareth, 11, 59, 61-66
   coarsening of, 63-64
   as cosmic teacher of peace and salvation, 59
   as a free spirit, 62
   his practice, 64-65
   as the redeemer, 59, 63-66
Jung, C. G., 5-6, 18-19, 23-24, 41, 135
   Nietzsche's Zarathustra, 23

Kali Yuga, 103
karma, 15
Kingdom of God, 62
Krell, David F.,
   Daimon Life, 131
Kreuther, Conradin, 119
Kühlewind, Georg, 92-93, 116-117
   Feeling Knowing, 92, 128
   From Normal to Healthy, 104
kundalini, 43-44

labyrinth, 23, 60-61, 65
lack of distress, 10
Lampert, 45
   Nietzsche's Teaching, 17, 45
life body (emotional body), xix
lifelessness, (soul's), 79

Lifton, Robert Jay, xx
light-beings, 47
light-force, 44
light of thought, 104
living and thinking. *See* thinking, living
logos, 144-145, 147
  as a language, 2, 9
  of the soul, 101-102
Lord Chance, 42, 44
love, xviii, 8, 12-13, 28-30, 33-35, 37, 39,
  51-54, 57, 59, 61-64, 68, 81, 85, 92, 94,
  99-100, 108, 118-119, 130, 132-134,
  138-139, 149
  cosmic-human-love, 35
  as cosmic light, 8
  love of fate. *See* Nietzsche, his *amor fati*
  self love, 28-29, 100, 132-133, 135,
  selfless love, 96
  sense-borne, love, 132
  spiritual love, 115
  universal love, 133-134
love of oneself, 28-29, 31-32, 35, 37, 77
Lucifer, 101-105, 134-135
luciferic, 101-103, 107, 134-135, 138

machination, 10
manic-depression, 137
materialism/materialistic, xx, 2, 6, 11-12,
  42, 54, 64, 66-67, 74-75, 84, 88, 90, 101,
  104, 129-130, 135, 137, 147
materialistic consciousness. *See*
  consciousness, materialistic
materio-metaphysical, 5, 119, 125
Maupassant, de, Guy, xx
maya, 42, 111
McKenna, Terence,
  Food of the Gods, 28, 45
meditation/meditative, xxiii-xxiv, 10-11,
  13, 15, 18-20, 25-26, 32, 35, 42-43, 81,
  87-88, 104, 116, 119, 138, 143
  Bird Flight Meditation. *See* Zarathustra
  (Nietzsche's), Bird Flight Mediation
  paths, xv
  practices, xxiv, 12, 36, 138
  retreats, 18
meditative silence, 87
meditative consciousness. *See*
  consciousness,

meditative
mediumship, 83
metamorphosis
  of soul, 8, 14, 47, 131, 138
  of thinking, 105
metaphysical/metaphysics, 1-2, 8, 40, 62,
  111-112
Michael, 12, 103, 105, 107
  age of, 105
  as Archangel, 12, 103
  as the Countenance of God, 103
  impulse of, 107
  as the luminous angel, 13
mineralization, 24
moral clairvoyant knowledge, 130
moral consciousness. See consciousness,
  moral
moral imagination, 94, 149
moral perception, 31
Munn, Henry, 47
mysteries, ancient, 130, 148
mystery centers, 46
Mystery of Golgotha, 11-12, 66-67, 103,
  136, 148,
mystery, sense of, xxiii-xxiv

narcissism, 28, 38, 56-57, 59, 85, 113, 132.
  See also love, self love
  fear of death, 135
Narcissus (mythological figure), 132
new consciousness. *See* consciousness, new
Nietzsche, Friedrich, xv-xix, xxi-xxii, 1, 6-
  8, 11, 15, 17-20, 22, 24, 27-33, 36-37,
  51, 53-55, 59-66, 68, 127, 148
  his *amor fati* (love of fate), xviii, 8, 17,
  32-36, 38, 57, 64
  The Antichrist, 7, 59-65
  Beyond Good and Evil, 7, 22, 30-31, 53-
  54, 62, 65
  Ecce Homo, 7, 19, 21-23, 31-32, 36, 51
  eight-fold path, 60
  existential psychology, 11
  The Gay Science, 1
  "God is Dead," 1
  negativism to the Church, 60-62
  philosophical psychology, 19, 27, 36, 44,
  66
  program of abandoning our mental

structures, xvi
seven solitudes, 60-61, 65
"The Three Metamorphoses," 7
"Thus Spoke Zarathustra," 7, 17-20, 35, 38, 41-42, 51, 53, 55, 59
transvaluation of values, 17
Zarathustra's "Eternal Return," 18-19
nihilism/nihilist, 7, 20, 25, 27, 30, 32, 36, 42, 53-57, 59-60, 64-68, 87, 118, 127-128, 130
noble/nobility, 29-32, 36-37, 54, 59
noble souls, 30-34, 36-37, 49, 54-55, 58-59, 65, 67-68

objects (of thinking), 114, 117
obsessions, xx
obsession with death, 78-79
O'Flaherty, Wendy D., 46
ornithological/ornithology, 18, 24, 34, 37, 41
ostrich, 29
Ott, Jonathan, 46
Otto, Rudolf, 132
    The Idea of the Holy, 132
    Pharmacophilia, 46
    Stages of Consciousness, 116-117
    Thinking of the Heart, 118-119
Overman, 7, 18, 27, 30-32, 34, 36, 41, 50-51, 68

Parmenides, 111
passion, xviii
pathos of distance, 31

percepts (of thinking), 114-115
perception, 26, 34, 88, 114-115, 117-118
    moral, 30
    sense, 70, 74, 95, 11
Persian wisdom, 51
Phantom, 134, 148. See also Christ, Resurrection Body
philosophical psychology, 7, 19, 32, 36, 44
pineal eye, 26-27
    transformed to celestial eye, 26-27
Plato, 131
Platonic Doctrine of Eternal Forms, 111
Platonism, 18
play, 7-8, 87

poet/poetic, 5, 11, 142-147
polarity-of-unity, xxii
prana, 43
presencing, 4, 10
pride, 41, 132-133
Prokofieff, Sergei O.,
    Rudolf Steiner and the Founding of the New Mysteries, 57-58, 111
potentia, xx
prototypal imagination. See imagination, prototypal
psychoanalysis, 75-76, 82, 88, 95, 132, 135. See also Freud
    depth psychoanalysis, xix
psychotherapeutic/psychotherapy, xiii-xv, xix-xx, 5-6, 14, 71-74, 81-83, 90-94, 96, 100-101, 103-107
    as a modern initiation practice, xix
    as queen of disciplines, xiii-xiv
psychotherapeutic conversation, 81-86, 89
psychotherapeutic encounter, 5-6, 14
pull-to-freedom, xxii
Pythagoras, 111

Rank, Otto, 30
    The Double, 135
reason, 112-113
redemption, 55
redemptive imperative, 54, 59-60, 65-66, 68
relational revolution, 3
reincarnation, 15
releasement, 10-11, 123-124
resonance/resonating, xvii, xix
ressentiment, 22
Resurrection Body. See Phantom.
revaluation of values, 7
revelation, 67
revenant, 41
revenge, 19, 22, 27, 34-35, 38, 53, 55-60, 62-65
reverence, 3, 21, 31, 55
reverent nobility, 61
Rig Veda, 46
root chakra region, 26
rootedness, 123
Ruck, C., 46
rupture in human destiny, 1-2

Sabina, Maria, 47
sacrifice/sacrificial, 19, 50, 58, 108, 149
Sardello, Robert, xxiv
　Freeing the Soul From Fear, xx
　Silence, 87
schooling of consciousness, 104-106
Schuré, 21
Schwartz-Salant, Nathan,
　From Sphinx to Christ, 21
　The Black Nightgown, 72
　subtle body, 71-72
self-centeredness, xiii, xiv, 65
self-consciousness, 1, 138
selflessness, 12, 55, 68, 87, 108, 119, 138-139
self-love, 28-29, 100, 132-133, 135
self-other-world, 18, 65, 74, 79, 124, 127
sensory reality, 114
serpent (Indian), 42-44
sexual, 35, 43, 75
　aggression, 137
　causality, 12
　ecstasy, 43
shamanic/shamanism, 46-47
　consciousness of, 47
　Mazatec shamanism, 47
　　its musical language, 46-47
silence, xvii
slave morality, 27
Socrates, 130
soma (sacred mushrooms), 46-47
　its symbiosis, 47
Sophocles, 111
soul anatomy, 101
soul consciousness, 129-130
soul experience, xv
sound and healthy love, 28
Spirit (Holy Spirit), 101
Spirit of Gravity, 17-18, 22-23, 33, 35, 38, 41
　as demonic force, 38
spirit experience, xv
spirit self, 94, 117
　"I am" as, 117
　as a primal spirit-being, 117
spiritual-philosophical, 110
spiritual psychology, xiv, xxii, 3, 33
spiritual science. See anthroposophy

spirituality, xiv, xxiii
Stambaugh, Joan, 7
　her evaluation of Nietzsche,
　The Other Nietzsche, 7
Steiner, Rudolf, xv, xvii-xix, xxi-xxii, 6, 11-15, 66, 69-70, 74-80, 84-89, 91, 96-119, 125, 129-139, 148
　Anthroposophical Leading Thoughts, 104-105, 131, 134
　Anthroposophy in Everyday Life, 77
　Archangel Michael Meditation, 13
　Building Stones, 11
　The Challenge of the Times, 96-101, 133
　"Christ at the Time of the Mystery of Golgotha," 66
　The Effects of Esoteric Development, 77, 133
　elective affinity, 97
　Evil, 136
　From Jesus to Christ, 148-149
　At the Gates of Spiritual Science, 137
　Human Tasks in the Higher Worlds, 137
　The Influences of Lucifer and Ahriman, 101-103, 134
　Intuitive Thinking as a Spiritual Path, 104, 113-116
　Love and Its Meaning in the World, 132
　Manifestations of Karma, 132
　Metamorphosis of the Soul, 131
　Michaelmas and the Soul-Forces of Man, 12
　The Mission of the Archangel Michael, 101
　new mysteries, 111
　"new yoga of light," xvii
　Nietzsche: Fighter for Freedom, xviii
　An Outline of Esoteric Science, 76, 111
　preparatory and supplemental exercises, 86
　program for social renewal, 96
　Psychoanalysis and Spiritual Psychology, 14, 76
　psychosophy, 140
　his reverse ritual, 97
　"Social and Antisocial Forces," 97
　Reappearance of Christ in the Etheric, 13, 15, 67, 74
　Reincarnation and Karma, 15
　Secret Brotherhoods, 136

The Secrets of the Threshold, 75
subconscious, 91-95, 97, 99-101
subject (of thinking), 114
suffering, xx, 22, 25, 37, 94, 106, 149
supersensible, 66, 72, 88, 105, 111, 130, 149
supraconscious, 92-95, 101
surrender, process, xix, 3, 70-71, 73
sympathies, 76, 98

taste, 30
temperments, four, 76
terror/terrorism, xiii-xiv, xx, xxiii, 2, 4-5, 8, 15, 20, 34, 44, 59, 87, 90-91, 100, 107-108, 110
time's desire, 55-57, 59
theoretra/theoretric, 80, 82
therapeutic initiation. *See* initiation, therapeutic
thinking, xvi, xxiv, 4, 24-25, 31, 42, 67, 76, 80, 92-93, 95, 98, 104-105, 107, 110-119, 121, 124, 135, 137
    calculative, 119-121, 123
    cartesian materio-metaphysical, 112
    head, 102
    intuitive, 119, 125
    living, 104-106, 108, 115-118
    materio-metaphysical, 112-113, 119
    metaphysical, 111
    meditative, xxiii, 104, 119, 121, 123-126, 143
    thinking about thinking, 116
    transitive, 110
    true (sense-free), xxiii, 104
thinking being, xxiii
thinking, feeling, willing, 19, 63, 88, 97, 102, 125
thought-feelings, 26
thought images, 105
thoughtlessness, 120, 125
threefold social organization, 97
threshold experience, 78-79, 84, 88
tolerance, 58
Tolle, Ekhart, xxiii
Torok, M., 80-83
    Theoretra: An Alternative to Theory, 80
    séance, 82-83
transcendence/transcendant, 17, 23, 25, 27
transference, 19, 93-94, 106
transformation, xviii, 5, 7, 14-15, 20, 37, 42-44, 47-48, 70, 74, 78, 84, 96, 111, 124-125, 130, 132, 142
transvaluation, 17-18
trauma/traumatize, xx, 70-72, 74, 78-81, 83-84, 86, 88, 94
truth of the way, 32
truthfulness, 8, 20, 36
Turanians, 21
Turner, Victor, 71
    From Ritual to Theatre, 71

universalization of terror, 2-4, 6, 8, 10, 12, 15, 39, 64, 67, 89-90, 126, 142, 149
unknown destiny, 35

Vahumanu, 21
vanity, 29
Vedas, 42
Vedic, 25

Waldorf education, 11
warmth of heart, 136-137. *See also Gemut.*
warmth-light, 26
Wasson, R. Gordon, 45-47
    "fruit-plants," 46-47
    The Road to Eleusis, 46
    Soma: Divine Mushroom of Immortality, 46-47
wholeness, xxi
will/willing, 22, 29, 31-32, 55-58, 64, 66, 76-77, 80, 86, 91, 99-100, 102-103, 118, 134, 136, 138, 147
will-to-will, 10
Winnicott, D.W.,
    his interfacial region, 71-74, 81, 83-84, 86
    Playing and Reality, 71
wisdom, 3, 8, 21, 30, 36-37, 51-52, 54, 85, 90, 94, 101, 111, 118-119, 130, 149
    cosmic-human wisdom, 54
    moral wisdom, 20

yield to unknowing, 71
yoga, xvii, 25, 43
Zarathustra (Nietzsche's creation), xvi-

xvii, 17-29, 31-32, 34-52, 55-56, 58-60, 111
as apostle of Ahura-Mazda, 21
animals, 40-41, 45, 48-50
art of becoming, 59
as Asjabr, 21
aura of rainbow colors, 50
Bird Flight Meditation, 25-26, 28, 41
disgust at man, 39, 48-49, 51
ecstatic flight, 23-24
fruit-plants, 45, 47-48
initiation, 21-22, 25, 38-41
music and money, 23-24, 37
as the Persian wisdom teacher, 20
Serpent Power Meditations, 42-44
taste, 30-31
as teacher of Eternal Return, 45, 49
"The Convalescent," 38
his teachings, 19